The Magic of You

Stepping into Your Cosmic Body

Lynette Leckie-Clark

BALBOA.
PRESS

A DIVISION OF HAY HOUSE

Balboa Press books may be ordered through booksellers or by contacting:

Balboa Press
A Division of Hay House
1663 Liberty Drive
Bloomington, IN 47403
www.balboapress.com.au
1 (877) 407-4847

Because of the dynamic nature of the Internet, any web addresses or links contained in this book may have changed since publication and may no longer be valid. The views expressed in this work are solely those of the author and do not necessarily reflect the views of the publisher, and the publisher hereby disclaims any responsibility for them.

This book is not intended as a substitute for the medical advice of physicians. The reader should regularly consult a physician in matters relating to his/her health and particularly with respect to any symptoms that may require diagnosis or medical attention.

Any people depicted in stock imagery provided by Thinkstock are models, and such images are being used for illustrative purposes only. Certain stock imagery © Thinkstock.

Printed in the United States of America.

ISBN: 978-1-4525-1173-3 (sc)
ISBN: 978-1-4525-1174-0 (e)

Balboa Press rev. date: 10/12/2013

Contents

Channelled Meditations

Channelling—
Master Kuthumi speaks

Master Kuthumi

When Master Kuthumi came to me in meditation I knew a different spirit guide was with me. I felt it.

I was born with the gifts of hearing, seeing, feeling and sensing— what I call the essence of spirit or a person or animal who has crossed over to spirit, so I asked the question—"Who are you?"

I couldn't even pronounce his name! However that was soon overcome as I learned about this spirit who wanted to work with me. Once I discovered just who Kuthumi was and that he was an Ascended Master, and world teacher of the ancient knowledge no less, I asked, "Why me." Kuthumi told me he had chosen me because I would be a clear channel for his work, which he needed. He said we had worked together before in a previous life time when he was Pythagoras, and why not me.

I am long past these feelings of self doubt now and over the years I have had the privilege, as have his students, to know him, and to love him. He can be blunt and straight forward, but you do get a clear answer to your questions. Kuthumi has taken me to various countries around the world over the years, to teach the ancient knowledge many say is new today. It is a great privilege and I have enjoyed the excitement of making wonderful new friends along the way.

Kuthumi is always with me. It's difficult to describe but I only have to think of him and he shows me his face. Interesting the face of my portrait of him. He was very particular about his eyes I remember, the colour.

We continue to work together as I am his chosen channel for the teachings and knowledge he brings to mankind through me. These are throughout this book which contains a great deal of knowledge for those who seek it. This book is our gift to you.

Lynette

"Through knowledge comes understanding,
and understanding releases fear."
Ascended Master Kuthumi

The Ascended Master Kuthumi is the door-keeper of the ancient Occult Mysteries, and is also the co-protector of the <u>Holy Grail</u>— the ancient quest for self-awareness.

Master Kuthumi will be instrumental in the re-emergence of knowledge that has been lost to mankind for so long.

He also endeavours to assist those who participate in religious instruction, encouraging all concerned to open the Heart Charka in order to express Unconditional Love to all.

Master Kuthumi currently shares the role of World Teacher. However, during the Age of Aquarius Master Kuthumi will take on full responsibility for this enormous undertaking.

In previous incarnations he was Koot Hoomi Lal Singh and attended Oxford University in the late 1800's. He was of Kashmir origin.

In another incarnation he was Pythagoras (582-500 bc) he established a mystery school in the South of Italy, which was mostly devoted to the teaching of Mathematics, Numerology, and Sacred Geometry. Founder of the Hippocratic Oath, the Tree of Life, and the use of a mandala. This school was destined to become a Mystery School for the White Brotherhood.

Another incarnation was as Balthazar, one of the Three Wise Men who came to Baby Jesus. And in yet another very well known incarnation he was Francis of Assisi. And again later as Shah Jenan, builder of the Taj Mahal.

In the late nineteenth century, Master Kuthumi, with Masters El Morya and Maitreya, was instrumental in the establishment of the Theosophical Society, to ensure that long lost truths re-surface.

Kuthumi's Personal Words To You

As the Earth witnessed the ending of one century and the beginning of the new, a great pouring of powerful energy was sent to the souls on your earth in order to begin the process of mass enlightenment.

Many felt this calling to their soul, and indeed those who answered have awakened, and are in turn helping other souls to develop and open themselves to their soul knowledge and purpose.

Their efforts are applauded by myself and my brothers of the Lodge.

There is much to be achieved and each of us here also have a role to play in achieving enlightenment of the earth.

It is hoped brother will walk with brother, peace will be the normal way, not the exception.

Music will be lifted to new heights through the heart, and this will provide some powerful healing to man's emotional, mental and physical bodies.

All forms of control, petty jealousies and hatred will be left behind.

This process has begun.

Many on Earth are now hearing our call to awaken to their soul purpose.

To begin the change within themselves, to teach the new race of souls coming through on Earth.

As these souls grow in number mass change will occur on the Earth plane to one of love, peace and brotherhood.

And so it is a great joy to reach many souls on your Earth plane through my channel called Lynette.

She was chosen for many reasons, and I can say has herself overcame many lessons, not all of them easy for her.

Do not fear this change on your Earth plane, please do not allow fear to guide you.

Through this link we are able to guide and help you through this transitional time you are experiencing.

We can provide you with clear insight, which will allow the self to define your choices.

It is hoped this will give you more understanding, for by learning and understanding you will conquer any fear you may have.

Master Kuthumi

Chapter One

The Most Powerful Energy

Let's begin by understanding the most powerful energy you have which is still part of you today. This energy has created all you are, all you believe, and all that you create. It has always been with mankind. Yet most people haven't given it any attention at all and have never thought how to use it wisely to their advantage—to assist them every day.

This energy has always been there throughout each of your past lives. Yes every incarnation and every experience you have ever felt. It is perhaps the most powerful energy force you know and many don't even recognize the power available at their finger tips. You have been told you are more powerful than you realize. Most people just brush this statement aside without fully comprehending its true meaning.

So what is this powerful energy I speak of? How is it that this energy force has gone largely unnoticed for so many centuries? Yet there were some who knew. Some who used this great power in quiet contemplation and used this energy to provide them with strength and even wisdom. The ancient wise ones knew about it and understood it. However there were many others, as history reveals, who did not fully understand this powerful energy, who strode blindly forward creating pain and suffering in their wake. Whether they understood this powerful energy or not, they used it in one form or another.

This great God given energy which allows you to create and to experience all manner of duality on this wonderful planet called Earth. This all powerful energy force which is there to teach you many things through your own choices as you walk your pathway of life, as you seek soul growth through inner peace and higher learning.

This powerful energy force so often overlooked is called the *Mental Energy Force*. What you think you create.

What do you draw to you?

So let me ask you what energy are you drawing to you? What type of people are you attracting to your circle? How do you speak, how do you reflect your inner feelings? How you reflect the image of yourself to the world is part of your life essence. Are you happy, sad, doubtful, insecure, confident? All of this and how you feel about *you* is your essence. Your essence reflects in the energy vibes you emit which will draw a certain type of person to you. Others see and feel your 'vibes.'

The ascended Master Kuthumi, who I work with, says,

> **Recognition is 80%. The other 20% is what you choose to do with the knowledge.**

So what you are drawing to you is a very powerful energy force—the *Mental Energy Force*.

What you Think You Create

This is your mental force. The force which you act upon. What you imagine continually you will create. Your imagination links closely to the mental force.

Your Beliefs

Sometimes you have a thought which links into the sub-conscious mind—the computer as I call it. The computer doesn't function on feelings. It simply acts on how you react to certain experiences. For example, if as you were growing up you were made to feel you had nothing important to say. This feeling would have been created by another's opinions, words and behaviour toward you over a number of years. You may have been continually put down for any opinions put forward. Made fun of. Others may have made jokes at your expense also. Later, a school teacher may have verbally torn one of your essays to pieces with words. An essay you spent a lot of time on and felt very proud of. This type of behaviour from others toward you would register in your sub-conscious mind, the computer, as "what I say is not important." These very words would be the *key* the computer lodged. As you grew up, at various times, the same exact words may not have been spoken to you by others, but the inference would be clear enough to hit that key in your 'computer'. The key to those words "what I say is not important," you have made your own belief. A belief that has grown stronger over time. This is a belief *you* have created.

You have heard of the expression, "He really pushed my buttons!" In other words, he really pushed some of the deep inner beliefs held in your sub-conscious mind. You can change this. You have a powerful force which helps you form your *own* beliefs. Usually in life the Universe sends you a trigger via a person or an incident which causes you to stop and think about your reaction to a certain situation. You may repeatedly be sent a 'messenger' until the day you finally decide, "I want to change that belief."

You still have another step to take however before you will actually *do* the steps to create change. You need to be *completely ready* to do so. Completely ready to change a belief you may have clung on to for years. Take a person who smokes and wants to give up as an example. Or a person who wants to lose weight. Neither will seriously do the work until they are absolutely ready. Until they are in the space of their own mental force. That mental energy force, that great power will propel them forward to determined action.

So you see it is *you* who chooses. The fact is the more you think about something and the more energy you give it, creates your *own belief.* The good news is you don't have to live with your old beliefs forever. As you experience life and grow you usually find you've outgrown some of your beliefs. You have become aware of the way you react and feel when an old belief 'button' is pushed. That belief no longer sits well with the 'new' you. The Universe will ask you to take a look at that old belief you no longer need.

Master Kuthumi has given an exercise to help you on your path toward self mastery. These are scattered throughout this book and all are given directly from Master Kuthumi. The first exercise is:

Write down *four* things you like about yourself. Then write down *four* things you would like to change about yourself.

Some of these could be a repetitive or a negative reaction, a habit you no longer need to experience or an old belief. Write down your plan and what you need to do to achieve this change? At the end of each week write down the progress you have made toward your goal. Keep these notes in a journal so you can reflect back on your progress and achievements after you finish reading this book. You may be very surprised.

Fake It till You Make It

What you imagine, you create. So the saying *fake it till you make it* can be useful. You can imagine how you wish you *could* react to a certain situation or fear. Visualise it in your mind. How does it feel? In your imagination its real isn't it? You're putting a particular scenario out to the Universe every time you imagine it in your mind. Slowly you begin to believe it and to create it in your daily life. The scenario links back to the old mental belief and through your *Mental Energy Force,* a new belief is born.

Negative ideas in your imagination will cause you to defeat yourself because you are accepting a false belief as if it were a fact. You could link back to "what I say is not important" as an example of this. So you can begin to understand how you have perhaps unconsciously accepted many false beliefs. The 'fake it til you make it' principle can be used as *"I'm gonna make it."* Pretending and believing you have made it until it becomes *your* reality. Buddha said:

> **"What you believe is what you will be."**

Two Important Times

There are two very important times. The present time and missed opportunities. I recall when spirit kept showing me Teresa of Avila. Signs appeared everywhere. I kept seeing her in the etheric field and was told by a psychic I had been Teresa in a past life. I purchased a book taken from Teresa's own words and read it. I felt a deep recognition and though it was written in old English I understood it all. Yet still I dithered and thought more about it all. Time passed and I did nothing. I'm sure you are aware that a popular book on the beliefs of Teresa of Avila was published. My opportunity which had been presented from spirit was lost. It became a missed opportunity. I'm sure most people can relate to missed opportunities. Can you think how your life would've been changed had you locked into your *Mental Energy Force* and acted on something which was repeatedly presented to you?

Each Year You Change

You change through experiences and through people who come into your life. What is important to you changes as well. You follow what you've been taught and you copy behaviour. When you first came into this world as a baby, you didn't know hate, jealousy, greed, frustration or feeling inadequate. You were perfect in so many ways. However you soon learnt. What was the first thing you did? You cried. You learnt that when you cried you got hugged, fed, dry nappies, attention. Even a punishment is attention to a child.

You began to form a picture based on your interpretation of how you were treated and how you were spoken to in those early years. Later you learnt your concept of money. Many formed the idea you have to work for your money, and work very hard for every dollar. After all, you weren't really a good person if you didn't work hard anyway. Sound familiar?

You heard somewhere about manifesting. Sounds a good idea. So you decided to manifest five thousand dollars. You began to visualize the money. You put it out to the Universe and the Angels. Time went by. But where's your money? It didn't arrive. Where is it?

It comes back to *key beliefs* placed in your sub-conscious many years ago—"You have to work hard for your money." You didn't work for it so you don't really deserve it. You're not good enough—another key pressed. Many don't talk about the *Mental Energy Force* or the key beliefs that you formed in childhood.

Tell me, how are some of those beliefs fitting your life now? Are you beginning to form your OWN truth now? There's a saying—the truth shall set you free. You are beginning to form a *new* truth? Your life will be transformed according to the truths you are prepared to accept about yourself and discarding those which no longer serve you.

A New Foundation

You're building a new *solid foundation*. It's time to evaluate what is good and what is not. What is not fitting comfortably—right now? What is *your* perception of YOU—right now? Building a strong foundation will *empower* you to be happy and confident. Say to yourself, "I want to have a solid foundation of beliefs." It's time to review, to take away the pieces and the beliefs you no longer need—and be ok with it. To say, "It's ok, I've grown and that old belief is now too limiting for me. I don't need that belief anymore. I now have a new powerful belief. I'm going to radiate out a new essence, a new me."

As you sift through those old beliefs, don't dwell on the negative. *Keep positive thoughts.* Don't dwell on repeats. Every time I find myself in an old negative mode of thinking I remember—*don't dwell on repeats.* Change to a positive theme of thinking and change the scenery of your mind.

Become your own caretaker. Gently and lovingly create the canvas to grow in all directions of your life. You're a good person. It's other people's opinions which have formed a negative belief in your sub-conscious which has lead you to think negatively about yourself today.

Why do you need to hold on so tightly to the old movies of your life? Ask yourself, why? What good does it do you? No good at all does it? You don't need to keep on hurting. There is a wise saying which is—

> **What soap is for the body,
> tears are for the soul.**

Tears wash away the pain. They cleanse and they refresh.

Soul Wash Meditation

For those having trouble letting go of old incidents, hurt or pain, this Soul Wash meditation will help wash away all the hurt and pain. You don't need to repeat the details, just bring the event to mind. Hurt has been retained in your heart and you have harboured this hurt and pain for too long. It's time to release it forever. Are you ready?

Sitting comfortably in a quiet, slightly darkened room, close your eyes.

Breathe deeply in through the nose *completely* filling your lungs, and exhale *slowly* through your mouth. Do this twice more before calling in your spirit guides or angels.

Breathing normally now feel your self relaxing more and more and becoming still.

Breathe.

Now bring just the event to mind. Remember you're not alone in this. Your guides and angels are right there with you, supporting you. *Feel* their strength.

Now, how do *you* feel about the event? Do you feel angry? Do you feel indignant about what happened? Do you feel like swearing? Express your indignation. Say to yourself, "how dare you." Express how you feel in your mind. Breathe.

Now say to yourself, "I will no longer accept this type of behaviour from others. I will no longer tolerate others treating me like that." This is Heart healing. Pause, breathe.

It's time to release the pain, time to heal. Begin to fill your heart with love. Visualize it and begin to feel the love. Keep filling your heart with love until you feel your heart will burst. Feel it. See the love as a soft, beautiful Pink Ray of Light. Bathe in that Light for a moment. Allow the Pink Ray of Love to spread out over you. Visualize it. *Feel it.*

Now forgive yourself for any blame or shame you may have been holding deep within. Often you have carried this very deeply for a long time.

Say,
"I now forgive myself totally."

Feel your forgiveness. *Feel the love* once more. Bring that love deep within you.

You now need to fully release and let go. You also need to forgive the other person who was involved in this incident. You *can* forgive them through compassion. It doesn't mean what they did or said was right. Understand this. But forgive because with compassion in your heart, fuelled by the love you have placed there, you are able to finally understand, to acknowledge and to finally forgive and release.

Feel your heart being cleansed and your soul being washed clean with compassion and love. Let the issue go.

Now bring in the Light. Visualize white Light all around you like a mist seeping into those once dark crevices where you have held the fear and pain for so long in your heart. See it—feel it. Feel the Light. Bathe in that Light. Stay as long as you need to.

When you're ready gently come back to awareness and open your eyes. Now give yourself a shake. That's right, a *gentle* shake. Shake out any remaining negativity from your auric field. The process is complete.

You can do this Soul Wash meditation as often as you need to. Sometimes once is enough. Sometimes you need to repeat it two, three or more times until you can feel a complete release. The number of times doesn't matter. What is important is that you are able to let go and fully release this incident along with the pain, anguish and the guilt it created within you. So keep repeating the Soul Wash mediation until you *can* forgive and bring the Light into the space that was once holding pain in your heart.

Quantum Psychics tells us there is a wholeness to everything. But you can't join in the wholeness until you heal. That's what the Soul Wash meditation is all about.

The Disconnect Button

Sometimes in order to carry on you develop within you a 'disconnect button.' You disconnect a fragment of yourself from a person or an incident. By saying with much energy—"I hate him! I don't like him," you begin to disconnect. You lose your compassion. You put up etheric barriers around yourself in order to feel safe. These barriers simply keep your wounds and your old fears isolated. You cannot heal while you keep maintaining these barriers with new hurts and pain, or by continually reviewing those past hurts. With each new hurt you add you make the barrier stronger. At this point you block any healing. It becomes similar to when you need to talk to someone to make something right. But it's hard. So you wait. You put it off. It keeps getting harder. Time roles by. Nothing changes.

By waiting you are sabotaging any healing effort for yourself. To heal means taking responsibility—for YOU! You need to change the way you think about yourself. Aren't *you* worth healing? Then take responsibility. It's time. Master Kuthumi has given an affirmation to help you with this.

> **A crisis is an experience that allows me
> to learn, to heal, and to grow.**

The Cave Aspects

Every one has a cave. Yes you do. You've told yourself on a deep level you need a 'cave' to survive. It's where you can hide in your mind. Where you can stew over incidents and relive them over and over. Where you can wallow in the dark waters of self pity. Where you can reside in old dark paradigms of behaviour. It's where you constantly choose negative behaviour, negative words, and negative thoughts. You live in the cave of misery at times. Then you top it all off by asking "Why me?"

You've used this cave for a long time. In a way it feels ok. You go to the cave each time you feel life's got too hard and everyone suddenly feels against you. When you think you're too fat, not good enough, being picked on, and criticized. In short you feel a 'victim'. You feel sorry for yourself and maybe angry too. So you enter the cave—your cave.

Language

You develop the caveman language. How much energy you put into the caveman language depends on how long you choose to stay in the cave. This is where you can really beef up the negative comments from other people. All those comments bordering on an insult or put down suddenly become a mountain and become the worst insult ever! Then at times you even add to it yourself. Someone says, "You did a good job on that essay." You reply, "It took me so long to do it, and I had to redo it three times."

You just put yourself down. What does it matter how long it took you to complete the essay, or how many times you re-wrote it? You felt you needed to get it right. Why put yourself down using the cave language? Sometimes it's hard to simply say "Thank you," and feel good in yourself. Maybe it's time for a new *key* belief.

Image

Shoulders hunched, head down, you radiate "Don't talk to me. Don't look at me either." That gives you an excuse to yell at them and to take your anger out on them. The negative energy radiated from someone in this state creates quite a large energy field and it's not a nice energy at all. Worse, some people have developed a 'cave' energy for so long it has become normal behaviour for them. This is so sad. The cave language has become their most used vocabulary.

Thinking

Can you recognize these words?
I hate my life.
I'm too fat.
I'm sick of this job.
I never have enough money.
I'm sick of this.
I'm not staying here.
You make me sick.
I can't believe I did that. I'm so stupid.

This is all cave vocabulary. You can feel the negativity as you read it and have you noticed with someone in the cave it's just never their fault? It's always someone else's fault. Mmmm.

Beware Of the Cave Virus

Have you also noticed when you stay around a person using cave language how easily you can catch the cave virus? It seems to just spread to you quite effortlessly. Suddenly you notice you begin to feel differently. You begin to feel angry—then horrors! You begin to hear your self using the cave language. Your facial expression has changed. You're suddenly frowning at everyone. Things begin to go wrong. Your anger increases. You go home, and guess what? You enter your own cave. Yes. The cave virus has even spread to your home. Those you live with are catching it too. As the cave virus settles to others around you, you go deeper into your own cave. You have now become a cave dweller!

Your shoulders sink deeper to your chest. Your chin sinks down. Your frown deepens as does your mood. All the old grievances rear their ugly heads. You leave the room slamming the door behind you. A warning to anyone thinking of following you to just leave you alone. You are going deeper into your cave to stew in negativity.

A Reflector

You reflect what you hear and see. If someone around you becomes angry it's easy for you to become angry to, particularly if it's someone close to you. They may snap at you because they're in a bad mood. You snap back only louder. You snap louder because you have to win. Someone criticizes something you did. You criticize right back—with a twist. You try to think of something bigger or better. Someone at the office gossips about a workmate. What do you do? You join right in. You have become a reflector. Reflecting what you see and hear. Only you add to it, because you have an inbuilt need to win and to be better.

So often people develop this cave behaviour without even thinking. Maybe it's time for a review. Because you need to be constantly aware of what's happening around you. You do have a choice. You don't have to enter your own cave. You *can choose* to move away.

If you notice a friend has entered their cave don't offer sympathy. To do this will only justify their behaviour. They'll begin to think it's ok to use cave language and to feed their anger by talking about someone else. After all your giving them sympathy and your saying it's ok. Worse, if you keep giving them sympathy you're in danger of catching the cave virus too. Before you know it you'll begin agreeing with them and maybe start using cave language. You need to be aware of where you *want* to be. I'm sure that's not in your cave or entering someone else's cave! But . . . . there is help available.

Leaving the Cave

How can you get out of the cave? The more cave language you use, the more energy you feed your anger and frustration. Your whole body changed in the cave. Your blood pressure rose. The negative energy may have caused your tummy to knot up, your muscles to cramp, and your jaw to lock firm from grinding your teeth. Your mental body got overloaded with so much negative energy you now have a head ache. Your emotional body is locked in negative energy too, placing you in a really bad mood. How can you move out of this? How can you begin to heal, to move forward and create change?

Before we leave this chapter Master Kuthumi has another exercise for you.

First make sure you use the affirmation

> **A negative experience allows me to change, heal and grow.**

Second, for the next week note *all* the cave behaviour you notice from yourself, or from another person.

Keep these notes in your journal. At the end of the week read your notes.

Are you surprised at all that you noticed? Makes you think doesn't it?

Chapter Two

Introducing The 'CAN DO' Button

Learn to recognize any of the previous symptoms. You can usually feel the change of energy within your body so try to learn to listen within. Feel what your higher self is telling you through your body.

You do need a ladder to climb out of the cave any time you choose. Can Do (Your name). Yes, of course you can. Begin by making a button out of card for your wallet or purse. In large letters, perhaps with red or gold pen, write

> **CAN DO (Your Name)**
> **Yes _I_ Can.**

You can outline the card in a bold colour so it's easily seen. Remember this is _your_ big 'ladder.' You need to be able to see it quickly when the cave comes into view. It's a powerful reminder to stop! To climb out of that cave, especially when it sneaks up on you or you need some confidence to achieve a goal. Our local politician used this method to help him achieve his goal, and it worked. He won! To help you even further, Master Kuthumi has given me another affirmation for you.

> **I focus on my purpose**
> **not my problem**

Problems can draw you inward, right into the core of the situation. A problem draws you into the ego self and often causes you to begin to doubt yourself and your abilities. So you begin to think you can't do it, it's all too hard. Poor me. Where have you suddenly arrived? Mmm, cave mode. Where's that ladder? Here's another ladder affirmation from Master Kuthumi.

> **I have no lack in my life**
> **I only have limitless possibilities**

It's a good idea to write these affirmations on a card or pretty coloured paper. Place them where you will see them as often as possible such as on your mirror, on the top corner of your computer or on the fridge. You get the idea.

These channelled affirmations are words of gold. Why? Because by using and repeating the affirmations frequently you become much stronger in your resolve to be happy with more confidence in yourself and in your life!

The Overcoat Tree

Have you heard the story of the overcoat tree? The overcoat tree is always beside your front door. It's a small bushy tree with lots of soft green leaves in a planter. Each day when you come home from work or from a stressful situation you experienced while out, remember to pause at your front door before you enter your home and visualise all your stress and anxiety as an overcoat you are wearing. Now visualise yourself taking off that overcoat and hanging it on the overcoat tree by the front door. Shrug your shoulders deeply to help re-adjust your energy field.

Now walk inside with a smile of gratitude on your face. Why gratitude? Because you just found another ladder and used it successfully. You are home. You have found a great life tool and you have so many limitless possibilities in your life now. Why wouldn't you smile?

With this in mind let's take another look at the cave language. Your own put downs—
I can't do that
I'll never have enough money
I can't afford that
I'm too fat
I'm not pretty enough
I wish I had another job
Why is this happening to me?

Listen to Your Words

You *can* turn this around. It's a matter of being aware of your words. *Listen* to what you're saying and the words you choose. Turn those words around, here's an example.

I CAN do that—emphasize the word 'can'
I HAVE financial abundance NOW.
I CAN afford that.
I AM beautiful. I LOVE my body.
I AM a good person
I *am THANKFUL* for this work experience.

You see. Not so difficult once you start listening to your self and your own words.

> **Change comes easily every day**

You are using cave ladders to turn your life around. I'm giving you the tools to achieve that. You can now choose a happier, positive life every day. You only need to focus on *one day at a time.*

Abundance Issues?

Do you feel others seem to have more than you? They may seem to achieve more, have more money and more material items including that great new car. You may see them as being more successful than you. Suddenly you begin to feel unsettled within. You begin to shrink inside, you feel inadequate and very unsuccessful.

If you stayed in this mindset it could easily grow into a huge block in your life. It would be the case of 'the molehill becoming a huge mountain!' You would soon feel quite weighed down each day. Your shoulders may physically become quite sore due to the burden you have created. But you know it's easy to focus on what *you* feel hasn't worked. Many are programmed to this thought pattern from childhood. Example—being constantly told, "You can't do this, you can't do that, can't you get it right, why can't you do it properly, why can't you get better marks, you'll never make the team". All continual put downs filtering into your sub-conscious to form a *key* belief about you! So when ever you have less in any area of your life your sub-conscious, the computer, remembers and notes that a key belief button has been activated. So unfortunately the cave begins to loom before you.

Sadly most of the educational systems are organized around what you get wrong. You are 'trained' to label yourself and your constant problems. Let's go back to our cave ladders and the five levels. You need to turn these negative key beliefs about yourself around and DELETE the 'put yourself down' button. That's right. Delete! Such a powerful word.

Here's an exercise given by Master Kuthumi:

Please take a look at what you've achieved in your life. List *four main ones*—boldly and clearly.

Write these on a card and put them in a safe place so you can read them when you feel down. This is a great exercise and a huge help in times of need. We'll talk more of this soon.

Turn Around Time

Let's begin. You need to remember that the way you think of yourself deep down has taken many years to become a key belief. Do you really think you need to keep holding onto the negative keys? No, you don't. So let's begin to turn those beliefs around.

Look at the achievements of your life. <u>ALL </u>of them. Write them down. Even the smallest. It's not just about the big ones. What about those times you helped someone else to do something and to achieve a desire they had. That's another of *your* achievements. If you just sat and listened to a friends problems, that's an achievement too because you helped them feel better. You took the time to do it and to care. That's a big achievement. So get writing. You may need another page but try to select four good ones for your previous exercise.

Are you beginning to get a better picture of you? I want you to keep this list you have made of your achievements and keep it in a safe place. To begin the turn around you need to read this list every day.

You'll begin to feel better and better about yourself. The four main ones on the card are for emergencies.

You are *deleting* your put down button about yourself. Don't stop reading your list. Just as it took time to form that key belief, it will take time to re write it. Not as long of course, but some weeks or even a month depending on your intent and self discipline. Keep it strong and positive and you'll achieve that turn a round in no time at all. Ask yourself, "What am I asking the Universe for?"

> **The Universe only obeys your words**

What are you actually attracting to you through your thoughts, words and re-actions? It is _how_ you react. This is where your learning is—the most potent learning in this life time. You have chosen to reincarnate on the planet at this time to be a part of the great shift of the Ages.

Coming Home to Yourself

Ok, at this point it's time to sit down and be really honest with yourself. No more excuses. We all find excuses for anything we perceive to be too difficult or too intense. So often the cave language begins. "I don't have time. I'll start next week. It's just too hard." So it goes on and that project gets put off until you feel, "It's just not for me."

This can happen when you decide to begin to learn about an aspect of metaphysics. You may choose to learn about a form of energy healing, meditation, spirit guides ect. Suddenly the ego self pops up into your mind and takes you straight into the cave. Self doubting thoughts flood your mind and you make excuses why you can't begin. You know, everyone has experienced this. What to do? Grab that cave ladder. Where is it? What page? (It begins on page 16.)

Great! Already you recognize you've entered the cave and are fast catching the cave virus! Be mindful of not allowing yourself to wallow and drown in self pity—oh poor me!

> ## I focus on my purpose

What was your purpose before that ego self plummeted you to the cave? What was it you wanted to do or learn about? **Like attracts like.**

Mental Magnetism

Think about what you're giving your energy to? What are your dominant thoughts? Because whether they're about happiness, sickness, self doubt, wants, higher learning or cave language, that's what you'll get! That's what the Universe will send to you. The Universe only obeys your words and your thoughts are words too.

You need to know *exactly* what you want in your life in any moment. Example. You may say frequently, "I want a new car, a Ford." That night you may change your mind and decide you no longer want a Ford. You now think a Holden car, or maybe a Dodge. What you want is a another car. But you are now undecided about the details. This indecision creates confusion for the Universe. It is very important to know exactly what you want and to be clear about *all* the details. What you focus on is what you get from the Universe.

Focus clearly on your thoughts, mind images and absolute success in achieving your desires. If this image changes you create confusion. Visualize the car, the make, model, year and colour. See yourself driving the car. If you're undecided on the details the Universe can not help you.

Mental magnetism only attracts your true wants—not your fantasies. Why is this? The answer comes back to mind power and the sub-conscious. Your inner plan of what you can truly have on a deep often hidden level. You may decide you really want to win the lottery. You buy your ticket. You visualize yourself winning. But it never actually happens in reality. You never seem to win the large amount of money you desire.

Hidden deep within your sub-conscious is the key belief of, "Well, I won't win anyway. I'm not that lucky." Mmmm. Know what? You have just cancelled out 80% of your focus. You see lodged into your sub-conscious were the words repeated over and over as you were growing up. "Now you must work hard in life. Nothing's free. You must work for every penny." You may think you've forgotten but your sub-conscious hasn't. You are now wanting money without working hard for it. So this now becomes one of those key beliefs that need to be turned around.

Play Make Believe

Remember the saying "Fake it til you make it?" It's really about pretending. Playing make believe. Why not pretend you've won some money. *Really feel it*. Think about what would it feel like to you? Focus on the important things you want to buy. How would you spend the money? Truly see your self over and over as being worthy of winning. Know it's now _your turn_ to win. It's *ok* to win a lot of money. Focus and believe. Believe in *you*. Believe you are *worthy* of winning. This is so important.

You may not want to win a lottery but the principles you use are the same. The focus is <u>essential.</u> There's a ripple effect of your thoughts. Just as when you throw a pebble into a pond it creates a ripple effect. So do your thoughts.

Positive Thought Waves

Did you know that positive thoughts set up thought waves that are bigger, more energetic and a stronger vibration? Yes, so it follows you will attain your goal much faster with positive thoughts because of this magnified effect. Positive thoughts are a more powerful, and stronger vibration. The energy of positive thought waves are longer which are carried out to the Universe. Science is now measuring thought wave patterns. One example are the photographs of water molecules. A molecule of water which is sent happy thoughts of love or is prayed over holds the shape of a snowflake. Quite perfect and beautiful. Sparkling and clear. Yet a water molecule with angry thoughts directed at it becomes distorted in shape and begins to change colour from white to brown. This has proved the energetic *mental power* of thought. Therefore how powerful is *your* focused thought?

You Are a Powerful Being

Negative thoughts of lack, poverty, un-wellness and resentment all create limitation of your power. You lower your energy magnetism of your mind and body immediately. These are limitations which you_have created. So what chance would you have to attract any of your desires with even a small amount of this limitation? You just used a lot of energy to create limitation.

Let's think about it. When you feel angry, resentful, in lack and sad, you usually become tired quite quickly. Negativity *destroys* your physical energy. It *breaks down* your vitality and worse, your mental power energy magnetism. But what to do?

Build Your Personal Tool Box

Learn to use one word. Keep it in your toolbox. That powerful word is **delete.** Say it. Louder. See how powerful it feels. You somehow feel stronger, in charge again and back on track. In those few short linear seconds of time which took you to firmly say delete, you switched back on your *mental power.* So that one powerful word allowed you to stop, pull back and take control. I can assure you this works!

Like everything you need to get in shape—mental shape. You need to practise using and feeling the power of this word, *delete.* Practise is best.

What are you bringing home to yourself? This is about *you.* Learning and growing. Practising and utilizing your full potential. Your full power that is your birth right. It's about *you.* When you're confident you become a magnet to other people. They feel a new energetic field around you. They see your vitality for life. But more than this, you become in charge of your life in every area.

You're in Charge

The not so nice remarks of others no longer have the same effect on you. You now have energetic mental power. You're in charge! You are now stronger to leave others negative comments or behaviours with those who sent them instead of taking them on board. You can now *choose* not to take them on board. You are no longer so weak that those negative words and actions sit in your consciousness wearing you down with worry and self doubt. You begin to build wonderful self confidence through this process as you release any limited potential through the power of your mind.

Practise and remember that key word delete. It's an effective switch allowing you to step into your positive mental power in an instant. *You* take charge. Now you can come home to yourself at the end of the day, the evening, or as you go to bed.

Let's summarize what we've covered so far. You are now aware of the cave and you are able to recognize cave language in yourself and others. You have become aware of not mirroring others negative emotions and of not entering into a ping pong game of angry words. Master Kuthumi has given you many affirmations to help you. Here's another one—

> **I am open to change**
> **I grow through a positive attitude**

You were given the Soul Wash meditation earlier to use when you felt bogged down in heavy energy, often from other people as the energy became trapped in your auric field. The cave ladder was given to help you climb out of any 'cave' situation.

You're beginning to re-programme the computer of your mind—the sub-conscious. You will notice some behavioural changes within you as well. Yet just like an athlete you need to keep practising to stay focused. But now it's the end of the day and I want to bring you home to yourself with a simple yet very short meditation.

Short End Of Day Meditation

Sit quietly and comfortably.

Close your eyes. Breathe deeply in and out three times. Feel yourself quite relaxed.

Take a moment to review your day. Not yesterday or tomorrow, just today. Keep it brief.

If there were any chores you had difficulty completing during the day ask they be completed quickly and efficiently.

Did you experience a challenge with another today? Say to that person 'I am sorry and I forgive you." Let it go.

Do you have a problem with someone? Ask how important is it really? Because in this peaceful review state you are allowing your higher self to take part so often you will be shown things a little differently. You will find the problem may not seem so important after all so you can simply let it go. If it is important then allow your higher self to show you a solution through a feeling, or by words dropping into your mind.

Simply say thank you. Thank you that you're safe, thankyou for your experiences today for each one allowed for your greater growth. Thank your angels for walking beside you.

You will feel now clear and at peace ready for a restful sleep.

This exercise only takes about five minutes of your time. Aren't you worth that? Of course you are and you will enjoy a peaceful sleep.

Chapter Three

Who Helped You?

You will now need a pen and paper. Please list the following:

Three teachers who really helped you through school.

Three people who taught you something worth while about life.

Three friends who helped you through a difficult time.

All of the people on your list made a difference in your life. They may not have made you rich, famous or successful. But these are the ones who really cared.

Are You Sabotaging?

I have a friend called Jane. On the outside Jane is successful. She has a great job as a receptionist in a large and successful company. She almost owns her home and has two healthy children aged 12 and 10. Her car is only two years old. Jane is a slim build and keeps herself well and attractive. She can chat happily on a wide range of subjects. Jane looks like the successful career woman on the outside but Jane can't seem to hold a lasting relationship. Time after time each union ends with the man leaving because Jane thinks he's not the one, he's just not right. I have to say I felt some of her boyfriends were lovely, very attentive, romantic, and more than one obviously adored her. "So what's the problem," I asked after boyfriend number 8! Jane replied, "They're just not right."

After a long chat with Jane I realized deep down Jane doesn't feel she's worthy of a happy, loving relationship. Each time a man fell in love with her and began showing her that love, Jane sabotaged the relationship. She placed brick walls around herself. She became distant within the relationship and began to pick quarrels. Jane felt deep down that she wasn't worthy of being loved. Because Jane had a very low self esteem she thought how could someone possibly love me? This had become a *key belief* and had its seeds in her childhood.

Sometimes when you hear a story like Janes it triggers some of your own inner feelings. If it does this to you, read Jane's story again. Be aware of *exactly* how you feel. Ask yourself why you feel like that?

Believe what you feel and are shown by your higher self. Give love to yourself. Lots of it and be kind to yourself. Recognizing a problem is 80%. The remaining 20% is taking steps to fix it.

Re-Building your Foundation

Together we're re-building your foundation. If a 'brick' in your current foundation is weak like one of Janes, then you need to let it go—now. Replace it with a new brick—a new belief that's stronger and better than the old one.

You have grown over the years haven't you? No one stays the same. Yet people try to go back all the time. Some go back to their home town after many years away thinking it will be the same as when they left, but find the friends and family members they knew are not be the same. Everyone has changed and moved on in their own lives. It's your mind picture that you have clung to. But it's a mind picture trapped in the past.

You have changed as well. People don't notice their own growth and change as much as they notice others. So your mind picture needs up dating. You need to allow growth in others as well as yourself. Often you look at your mind picture of the past and the people involved through 'rose coloured glasses.' You keep it that way affirming that picture over and over in your mind. Usually the Universe sends an event or an incident that causes you to take off those rose coloured glasses and see the truth. That's when you see things differently including the people involved. Affirmation . . .

I grow through positive change.

The inner reflects the outer. You grow and change through events and people who come into your life. You notice when a friend or your partner's reaction to your problems change. You begin to feel indignant and insecure. You plan an attack! You get angry and head straight to the cave. You challenge, "What's wrong with you?" from the cave. Your outer world has changed—but has it? Haven't you changed as well?

At this point you haven't altered your mind picture or your expectations. You feel you aren't getting the attention you deserve, nor the sympathy and caring remarks you feel you need. The word here is you. *You* feel. *You* need. This is *my* cave. It's all about *me*! What *I* want. *I* need attention. *I* need caring words. *I* need.

The outcome of this situation will depend on the other person's reaction. You are not only expecting them to be the same as they were in the past but you are also very neatly passing on responsibility. Responsibility for you feeling cared for, the attention you receive, sympathy toward you, responsibility for *you* feeling good.

Now we're at the core and it's about responsibility. You want to pass the buck. Well sorry, you can't. You can try. If you're a strong personality or very manipulative you may get what you want. An emotional fix—temporarily. But it will have a cost in the foundation of your relationship and whether friend or partner, the effect will be the same. At this point you need to stop and take four steps-

1. Ask how *they* are feeling?
2. Can you help?
3. Say, "Let's talk about this. I'm feeling out of sorts as well".
4. Share and heal.

Four easy steps to end conflict with a loved one before it really gets started.

How do you Relate?

I feel humans have lost the art of relating to one another. Not just talking, relating. How are these different? When you talk, you chatter so you don't have to reveal the inner you; you don't have to say how you feel within. You don't have to say what you *really* want, what you *really* need. Yet these are the three main things in any relationship which assist in creating a good flow of energies.

Think about what you want from the relationship, whether it's friend, lover or a work relationship.

Next think about how much of the inner you you're prepared to reveal to the other person. Are you already building walls around you because you think you need them to survive?

Finally think about what it is you actually need from this relationship. Is there anything? Is it your job? Your home? If the latter two are your needs you really need to sit and think about things as the situation could easily blow into emotional blackmail from your perspective.

In any relationship if you want it to survive and to have a solid foundation you need to be prepared to reveal your self. All of you. Don't try to cover up by being a servant to the other party and always trying to please another. Caring more about how *they* feel than how you feel. That will never be a satisfying relationship. Never! Yet you'll tell yourself, "This is my role. I feel better when I do everything for him/her. It keeps the peace" The relationship is sadly out of balance. Eventually you'll get annoyed because *your* needs aren't being met.

This can build up over time to a form of depression. You regurgitate the events and feed your inner anger. You decide you want out and you're not happy. On a deeper level you'll sabotage the relationship if the other person doesn't want you to go.

So you leave and suddenly you're free. You should be happy but you're not. Why? Because you still haven't taken responsibility for yourself. If you choose not to, you will repeat the same relationship and the same issues involved. Yes, it may be with someone else and a different place, but the unaddressed core issues will remain the same. That's why some people go from relationship to relationship and never find happiness. They will say, "Oh he turned out just the same as my ex." Let me explain why this occurs.

Beware of Repetitive Patterns

Unfortunately it all got too hard and you found it difficult to take responsibility for your part in the relationship. So you never learnt anything and you certainly never achieved the lasting happiness you craved. You needed to stop and look at the main points of a good relationship. Were you afraid of revealing the true inner you? What did you really want from the other person? Remember all relationships are a two way street, not a one way street. You need to take responsibility for your own happiness. If you're not happy with you, how can you expect anyone else to be. You *both* need to relate honestly with one another about your expectations, your wants, and your inner feelings. You shouldn't overlook a potential problem early in the relationship because you think you 'can change them.' No, and how rude of you to want to change someone else. You are only responsible for you—no one else! As Gandhi said—

> **Be the change you want to see in the world**

You need to build a strong foundation in any relationship if it's to last. So whenever a problem arises for either of you, you can sit down and talk about it honestly. Half truths and glossing over core issues won't solve anything for the long term. Say it like it is for you. Say how you feel.

Listen; really listen to the others point of view. Don't interrupt or talk over them. Give them the respect of listening to their words and concerns. You know 70% of people don't really listen to what another person is saying. How many times have you said, 'Oh yes," thinking you heard, but later discovered they actually said something different? Somehow you missed hearing a word, or in your mind replaced it with something else. It happened so fast you didn't even notice. But you heard what you *wanted* to hear. Listening correctly is a skill. You may need to focus on truly listening for a while. You might be amazed at what you actually hear.

So let's go back to needs for a moment and I'm not talking about material needs. You may need someone who treats you as an equal in a relationship. Or someone who will really listen to you and who will be considerate and loving. There are all forms of love. There's the love you have for a pet. The love you feel for a child, a friend, a partner or a parent. There's Universal love. All kinds of love. Someone who really loves you will accept you just as you are warts and all so to speak. But can you love yourself the same way? We began with asking what do you draw to you? Who are you attracting to you? How do they see you? How do you see yourself? That's important because how you see yourself matters a great deal in any relationship.

A New Awareness Grows

All of these issues relate to energy in one form or another. You have had thousands of lifetimes relating to lower third dimensional energy issues. Those previous experiences remain in your soul memory. If these are combined with feelings of lack in this life then it's very easy to stay locked on the lower levels of behaviour and to have poor self esteem.

Yet you have the power and the ability to change, to turn and raise your expectations, and to release old paradigms of behaviour. What we have discussed so far is to help you become aware of what patterns and core issues you no longer need. Never be afraid to let go and move forward. This is the way you make room for the Universe to bring you something or someone better in your life. These chapters are about guiding you along the path toward a new higher consciousness. To understand your own higher energy vibrations within. This is achieved through higher learning and a new awareness. So stay with me as we journey on together.

Tending your Inner Garden

I'd like you to visualize in your mind a patch of garden. The size doesn't matter. This is *your* garden so it's helpful to remember it.

In this garden there are some beautiful flowers of all colours. Red, yellow, purple, pink, white. Take time to visualize these colours in your garden.

Visualize how nice it looks, how colourful, and peaceful. Choose your favourite flower and study it closely in your mind. Look at the size, the freshness, the perfect petals and unique form.

Look at the stem. See how strongly the flower is connected to the stem. Notice if the stem is solid and well able to carry the perfect bloom.

Hold onto the image. Remember it. This is *your* flower in *your* garden.

The flower represents *you*. The stem represents *God* or who you perceive as God, for God is all things. The connection, the strong link between the stem and the flower is your guardian angel. The one who continually walks with you on your path toward fulfilment.

Master Kuthumi Speaks on Enlightenment

Master Kuthumi gives these words:

> *My dear Chelas, you hear this word soul often now, though it wasn't always so. Not so long ago people thought it a very strange word and many simply dismissed it. Did they think in*

their darkness with limited Light that they could dismiss their soul so easily, their mission, their purpose?

Of course this reaction was from the ego self. For it too was little understood. It was thought the conscious and the sub-conscious was all there was in the mind and in daily awareness.

Can I say to you that as you understand your higher cosmic conscious which is a part of the Light, you must release all past emotions from situations and experiences for they are now completed. They have been experienced. Why do you seek to torture yourself by keeping old negative emotions alive?

Enlightenment is releasing the emotional body from the past, from your present and your future. This may surprise you, yet I say to you, you can only be responsible for yourself and your own thoughts, words and actions. Not for another, no. For the children and animals you are a guardian, the protector until they are able to stand alone and begin to create their own experiences and choices.

You release with love and in strife turn away. Anger, jealousy and fear have no place in your Higher Heart. To become enlightened you flow from the Higher Heart and the higher power centres you call chakras or vortexes and then are able to flow from a higher consciousness.

I say to you as I walk among many in the coming weeks of this year viewing mankind's steps of transformation, you also will transform if you can walk the path.

Kuthumi

Wow! What a powerful message. But getting back to your flower and stem. I asked you to remember the vision that your higher self had shown you to give you hope and strength when ever you need it. We are in transition times and not everyone is at the same vibration and understanding. When you are faced with a grumpy customer for instance, or you are having a bad day simply remember your flower. Remember your guardian angel or spirit guide. Just allow that vision to uplift you, to carry you over that hurdle in the Now and to keep moving forward.

Releasing the 'Weeds' Exercise

Getting back to your garden, here is another metaphor. As you remember the over view of your flowers there are also some weeds. Some will be large, others small. Each weed represents an emotional block from your past created from a negative experience.

Pause for a moment, breathe deeply, and see how many old negative experiences your higher self presents you with. You need to allow this process to occur. Be honest with yourself. Just allow your higher self to guide you. Relax and calm your mind. Be still.

What do you see? What can you feel?

Know that whatever your higher self is presenting to you is for your highest good. It's time to release, to let go, to take back your power from the experience shown to you. Let it go.

You need to be free, ready for the exciting adventures ahead of you in these times of great transformational changes. These 'weeds' need to be pulled out from your emotional body. It's time now and you need to fly.

Take time to work through each experience presented to you. There is no need to relive any of these experiences in your mind. You've done that numerous times already. You just need a simple overview. There are two more methods I will cover. The first involves a person who has played a major part in creating the pain which you have long held onto. Here we go. Ready?

An Emotional Clearing Meditation

Sit quietly. Breathe in deeply, filling your lungs with air and slowly release through your mouth. Repeat this three times. Feel yourself now calm and peaceful.

Call in your angels and spirit guides and ask them to help you now. You begin to relax more now, feeling safe.

Call the person to you in your mind who you feel created the pain you have felt for so long. You can simply use their name only if you wish. Your angels and guides are still with you.

Now you can say what ever you want to say. You can go mad; even swear at them if you want. Release that anger and pain. Tell them how you feel.

Now forgive them because they didn't know any better. They were in darkness with no Light to show the way. Their energy and thoughts were dark because of this. If this weren't so, they wouldn't have hurt you so deeply.

Call your angels in close and visualize a small boat at the shore of a vast sea. Place the person involved in the boat and send the boat off to sea. Ask the Universe to take care of them.

Try to send unconditional love at this point. This will help greatly in your release process.

Now fill the space on your emotional body with love. See the soft and loving Pink Ray of Light washing over you, filling you with Divine love and inner peace. Take time to really feel this. You are sending this to yourself and you need every particle of this energy. Just rest quietly and peacefully. Thank your guides and angels for helping you with this process. It is done—finished. Rest. Breathe.

When you are ready open your eyes. Notice how different and lighter you now feel.

The second method is used for a block *you* created. Yes, you. Have you been shown something in your life you feel guilty about? Something you've been trying to hide for many years. Trying so hard not to think about it. Time to clear your guilt closet as well.

I Love Me Meditation

Sit quietly. Become aware of your breathing. Deep and slow.

Call in your angels and spirit guides and ask them to help you with this clearing.

Completely fill your lungs breathing in, then slowly breathe out through the mouth. Repeat this three times.

Bring to mind the incident you feel guilty about.

No need to relive the incident. Just tell your angel or spirit guide that you are so sorry you did . . . (event) You now see it was wrong. You are very sorry and you have learnt from this experience. You are sorry and apologize to anyone that was hurt by your actions or words at that time.

Say, "Please forgive me." Feel this from your heart.

Now ask the angel to take your hand. Visualize it. Breathe. Calm yourself by their presence. Breathe.

Now say from your heart with love," I now forgive myself." Your angel or spirit guide is with you. They know and understand that you must now release the guilt so they shower you in unconditional love to help you.

You now need to wrap yourself in unconditional love. Visualize wrapping yourself in a pink blanket of love. Feel safe, secure, loved, and finally released from the guilt you have held within for so long.

Breathe. Relax.

Thank your guides and angels for helping you with this process.

Now visualize a lovely white pyramid coming down over you. See yourself safely inside, protected in the Light.

It is done and completely released. Notice how much better you feel and how relieved.

Awareness of the Present Moment

Awareness is when you come fully into the present moment. There is only the present. The now! Weeding your inner garden is important. Some experiences are better than others. As humans we tend to hold onto the negative and often forget the good ones. Master Kuthumi says:

> ## As long as you have learnt, the experience is worthwhile.

That's why you incarnated here after all, to learn through experience. It's not the situation that matters. It's how *you choose* to deal with it. That's the learning. The soul growth.

Some people busy themselves with work and with life. They'll tell you, "I prefer my life this way." What they don't tell you is, "It stops me from thinking and it stops me from feeling." When they do stop they notice lots of things they never noticed before. It might be the things left lying around the house and not put away. It might be your partner who forgot to pick up your magazines or the dry cleaning. But you stopped and you noticed.

You become angry and critical. Some of your 'buttons' get pushed and you head for the cave and cave language. It's not long before your partner catches the cave virus. Maybe you don't care because the walls are crashing down around you and all because you stopped being busy. You suddenly noticed what's been there all along. You just never dealt with it. You chose to stay busy and avoid it.

Yet nothing's changed. So your busyness was a blanket that hid reality. It hid all the itty bitty things around the house. But now you've stopped and you've noticed. What do you do now? Where's that cave ladder gone? 80% is recognition. "I'm in the cave. I've got cave language." You're feeling sorry for yourself. Your partner shouldn't offer sympathy either. You have created this through your own choice and your own actions. You've been hiding behind; I'm too busy to notice! Time to take responsibility. The affirmation to help you move forward and deal with the situation is—

> **I focus on my purpose
> not my problems.**
>
> **I have no lack in my life
> I only have limitless possibilities**

So what are your limitless possibilities from this scenario? That's what you have to ask yourself. Write them down with a calm mind and an open heart. These are the two essential elements of awareness to enable the first stage of inner healing. These two elements give you the tools to work things out in your mind. To think over your priorities. To ask yourself just how important is your magazine, or your dry cleaning, or things not being put away? How important are these things in the bigger picture of your life?

Could it be you're stressed from work? Could it be you feel under pressure? Could you compromise with your partner on picking things up and putting them away? Look at the bigger picture without being swept away by negative emotions. You can't change what has happened, your reactions or your visit to the cave. But you can learn from it, and change. This meditation is very fast and can help in various situations. The more you use it the easier it will become.

A Two Minute Calming Meditation

The first step is about creating a calm mind again and coming home to you. First notice how you're breathing. Has it returned to normal breathing levels? Gently come back to your centre. Now close your eyes.

Breathe in slowly and deeply through the nose whilst visualizing white Light.

<u>Completely</u> fill your lungs breathing in, then slowly breathe out through the mouth. Repeat this three times. Now breathe in bringing that Light energy down to the bottom of your tummy, circle round and take any stale energy up and out through your mouth.

Now breathe normally. It is done. It may take a few minutes for the clearing energy to filter through to your physical body. Just wait and you *will* feel calmer. The secret is to fill your lungs with so much air while visualizing the Light energy that you feel your lungs will burst!

You can use this method for any debris left on a cellular level following a stressful situation. It's really good to release upset emotions and to restore calm within you.

The Higher Perspective Meditation

Another meditation to do when you're under stress, in a crisis, or have an agitated mind is this one.

Close your eyes and calm your mind. Complete the previous three breath method and relax the physical body.

Move your focus to your outer life and the happenings outside of yourself. Remember the inner reflects the outer.

Take a higher view of what's happening out there. Think of your flower. Bring it to mind. Visualize the flower, then the stem. Visualize a strong connection to your guide or angel. Take time to feel the energy of their presence.

What do you see? What do you feel? Have you been shown a higher perspective? A solution? Your higher self *will* guide you.

This can be through a feeling, a word or a vision.

When you're finished give thanks
Then visualize bringing a beautiful clear pyramid over you for protection from unwanted energies.
Now open your eyes.
You are now present once more.

This one really puts things into perspective. You may need to practice these exercises a little, but it is really worth while. You'll be glad you did. These two methods can become a corner stone to staying in charge of your emotions, and your life situations.

Overcoming the emotional body is considered man's greatest lesson by the Ascended Masters. You can perhaps now see why. Whenever you feel you need to use the cave ladder you can also focus on any of the affirmations given that you feel will help move you forward again.

> **I focus on my purpose.**

What is your purpose right now? Centre and become focused on *you* not someone else. Not their anger, their negative emotions or their issues. By focusing on *you*, you take your power back. You're in charge again. Clear and free to choose what and who you want to experience in your life. When you buy into someone else's opinion, anger, dominance or criticism, you give *your power* away.

You need to *choose* to centre. Choose to reconnect to your higher self and your higher wisdom contained in your soul. Next, choose to liberate your scars—the weeds—and to pull them out one by one. Live your life from the inside out. Not the outside in. Stay in your power. That's part of becoming free. Don't allow outside influences to control you and be mindful of not submitting to your inner demons.

When you take charge, you start living in the now. Those weeds in your inner garden took seed and grew—yesterday! How can you focus and live in the now when you're so busy giving all your energy to yesterday? So let's look at what you're giving to you.

> ## What are you giving to your soul?

Makes you think doesn't it? But let's just look at a scenario many can recognize. You experienced a deep hurt when you were twelve years old. You felt it, fed it over the years and rebelled because of it as you were growing up. Over the years you relived it again and again because either someone pushed that 'button,' or you activated it by doing something which triggered the memory. The scar on your emotional body grew thicker and stronger as time went on.

This quickly grew into a very strong weed. You kept feeding it energy so it grew and over time it grew into a huge 'block'. Did you realize if you don't deal your emotional blocks in this life time they grow even bigger and are carried over into your next life? Ouch!

So you can see the importance of learning to become a good gardener of your inner garden. It's time to look at your weeds. Look at what you're feeding your soul.

Chapter Four

What do you Appreciate?

We live in a beautiful place in Australia where many birds, mostly parrots, visit frequently. They feed on the variety of fruit trees and love the bottlebrush tree outside our kitchen window. We also have white and black Cockatoos who love to loudly screech their arrival in contrast to the silent Satin Bow birds that forage on the ground. The Rainbow Lorikeets chatter endlessly when the Guava tree is in fruit. They have a bright green back and wings, yellow and orange on their tummy, with blue and red around their neck and heads. Their wonderfully coloured plumage must be how they got their name.

I realize just how wonderful this is, particularly when I'm at the kitchen window and look up to see six or eight Rainbow Lorikeets loudly chattering while feeding on the sweet nectar of the red bottlebrush flowers.

My point in sharing this with you is telling you that I really appreciate this wonderful abundance of nature's beauty. But would I appreciate this as much if I'd always had this view of these birds? Perhaps not. They may have moulded into the backyard of my mind. My awareness and appreciation may not have been so great.

This is part of gratitude isn't it? What about you? How do you see your self at this point in the book, particularly after learning to become a good gardener? Is your perception of *you* beginning to change? Are you in appreciation of you? Do you notice all the wonderful things you have done for others and all the things you still wish to do? Do you see your own beauty? Do you see and acknowledge your soul now?

For some this will be a new experience. A giant step forward in their soul growth and awareness. They understand more of higher wisdom now and can understand the steps required to clear their past and emotional bodies. For others, it will be a return of remembering their soul in a life that just got too busy. It was too difficult to make the time to do the work. Another affirmation for you to use

> **I always make time for**
> **what is important to me**

If this is you, you probably feel guilty at this moment. Guilt is a negative emotion which many seek to hide within themselves. Guilt causes stress, anxiety and negative pictures in your imagination. Know you don't need it!

But sadly you've been made to feel guilty about a lot of things. When you arrived as a newborn babe you had no guilt at all. You learned the emotion of guilt. As a child you were constantly reminded of your bad behaviour, often made to feel guilty about what you did, and how you did something. You may not have been consciously aware of feeling guilty but your sub-conscious mind noticed and logged it into the 'computer' of your mind.

This also created a need to seek the approval of others. Some use the emotion of guilt all the time as a manipulative tool. All they have to do is to make you feel guilty. Since you've been conditioned to seek the approval of others that is not a difficult task. You seek the approval of the manipulator by doing what they want, or by doing what you think will make them happy, thus gaining their approval.

Manipulation from Others

Women often use sex as a manipulative tool, or a form of punishment with their partner. For example, you went for a drink after work. Your partner's not happy. So, no sex until she feels in charge again and thinks you've been suitably punished.

Sometimes a boss will use your fear of losing your job as a manipulative tool. You know you need your job. You need the money to feed your family. What will your partner say if you lose your job? A triple manipulation dump on you.

You can all recognize this I think in various situations. So my question to you is, how much energy are you prepared to give to your manipulator?

Not a lot I hope because what you decide equals your *power quotient*. Do you give away all your power or do you keep some and try to balance, often not very successfully—just because? Because why? Not just because your boss or your partner is making you feel guilty or fearful. No. Because you *allowed* it. You gave your power to them. You see the manipulator or the emotion of fear can only affect you if you *choose* to allow it to. You have all learned this behaviour. You have all experienced it. But now you have the opportunity to turn it around. To no longer let these scenarios affect you. You don't need to keep experiencing these emotions and loss of personal power any longer. You have a choice. This book gives you the tools to raise your awareness above many manipulations and inner fears.

Your Unlimited Potential

Once you understand you do contain within you <u>*unlimited potential*</u> you no longer need to impose feelings of guilt on yourself and you no longer need to judge yourself so harshly. You may beat yourself up mentally because you perceive you did something wrong. You go over and over the situation in your mind creating new scenarios each time. But it doesn't change the situation. Yet you verbally whip yourself some more. The situation doesn't change. It can't. It's happened. You need to accept this fact.

There are two things which will help. First ask what can you learn from the situation and the experience? There's always something. Be honest. It may be that you vow to yourself never to repeat it. That's still learning.

Secondly ask yourself just what is it that you feel guilty about? Once you know what it is you can make amends. Either to yourself by now having a better understanding of the event, or if you need to, make amends to another and apologize to them. If they choose not to accept your apology understand that is *their* choice.

That doesn't mean you have to keep on and on apologizing. The matter is finished when you take responsibility and decide to apologize. What the other person chooses to accept is their responsibility. Actions follow thought so gaining awareness of your own thoughts and words is a huge step on your path toward a new you. Of **becoming all you can be**.

In previous lifetimes man was often ruled by his ego. There are remnants of this in your soul memory. This makes ego behaviour seem familiar. That's why it is sometimes hard to turn old behaviour patterns around. Those old themes have been repeated over many lifetimes of experience. All the while you struggled to find the Light, a ray of hope.

Now you have the tools and a new awareness, a new understanding. Many are learning to turn away from behaviour ruled by ego. Yet you also need to understand your ego as well. This is sometimes described as your shadow side. It is necessary to integrate your ego into your entire being by understanding and being aware of the negative side of your ego. This understanding brings balance within as well as soul growth.

Your ego is necessary as your ego controls your fight or flight response. New understanding is giving you wings to fly free of old restrictions. With everything in life, what you think, what you feel, what you choose to do and how you act you and you alone are responsible for. God gave you freewill to experience and to learn from the choices you make in any situation. This enables you to experience free will. Sounds great doesn't it? The catch is it's tied to one word—responsibility.

As a child you learnt from your mistakes. When something turned out wrong you learnt not to do it again. You didn't get all caught up in it. You didn't beat yourself up over it for days, weeks or years either. You moved on. Life was simple then. So what happened? What changed? You grew up of course. But aren't you supposed to become wiser as you grow up? The answer is yes—if you allow yourself to be. Somewhere along the way that guilt feeling sneaked in along with a busy mind. But it's up to you isn't it? You have the choice.

You've heard the saying many times, you create your future. You do so by what you choose. Often how you choose to react to a situation, an experience. You choose. Master Kuthumi says;

"Spirituality is simple. It is man who chooses to make it complicated."

It's time man got back to the simple truths of life. Just as you did when you were a child. Back then you simply accepted and moved on with the business of growing up, of living and being happy.

Simple Acceptance of Yourself

This is needed by you now. Acceptance of yourself. You knew you needed to gain higher knowledge otherwise you wouldn't be reading this book. The first step is accepting yourself mistakes and all. Shall I tell you something? Master Kuthumi has said for many years that there are no mistakes. There is only experience. That's very true. You can truly understand Master's statement once you begin learning about the higher truths. It's from your experience you learn and you obtain soul growth. And did you know that knowledge stays with you life time after life time? The soul never diminishes. It only expands and grows.

Yet somewhere along the way you learned to look for everything outside of yourself. Looked to others to do things for you. Looked to others for love, to tell you what to do, how to respond, how to feel secure. Many feel they need someone else in life in order to feel secure.

As a soul before you incarnated none of these issues mattered. You were fine. Yes, there was your soul family around you in the Ethers, what many call Heaven. You were happy being independent *within* the whole. No one told you what to do or how to do it. You had integrity and you were true to your soul because you resided in a place of total love.

When you chose to give your power away to others you became dependant on them. You entered a separate state of thinking, of being. So you began to think you weren't responsible for your decisions or actions. The feeling of being separate grew. You continually looked to your outer world for all your needs—even your emotional needs. Do you see?

Freedom from all Lack

You wish on a deep level to be free. You know and feel there is something more. Your soul pushes you forward to seek, to find and to understand. You now desire freedom from your self imposed lack in all areas of your life. This requires new knowledge and self discipline. It requires responsibility. You will need to be quite observant as you seek to turn form your old ways, listen to your words and observe your actions. Write down what you notice. I suggest you try this for a week. I think you'll be quite surprised.

The Reward is Worth it

You may think that weeding your inner garden is tedious work. Often it is difficult. But the more difficult it is to erase a 'weed', the greater the learning. Remember that. It's true. Don't try pushing down memories that pop into your mind at odd times. Look at them. What and who are they tied to? Why do you need to keep a negative and painful memory within you? It's another layer to be peeled away. To be released from you. All the while you are feeling more and more free of old limitations. That's the reward. Freedom.

You can see now why this work is so important. Each step is layed out before you. The path of the disciple is not always easy but the rewards are enormous. It really is imperative you do the work in clearing your emotional body. You know if you don't deal with this now you will carry it over into your next life, and the next, and the next. It will keep you held down on a lower vibrational level until, perhaps in another life; spirit will again set the wheels in motion and place the right people on your path to enable you to gain greater freedom through release.

You do this for yourself, no one else. You know it's time. Your higher self has drawn you to this book and these words. This wisdom will give you the tools for what you want to achieve. Your ego has tried to pull you away, perhaps many times. By this point in the book you will have a greater understanding of this and will be aware of not allowing that to happen—again. No more excuses. Also understand that your ego will seek to pull you away from a higher path using a number of methods. The Cave Aspects are a favourite. Here the ego will seek to undermine your confidence. The ego is lazy and seeks to keep you just as you are at a lower level.

The ego can also communicate with another person's ego. So another person may turn away from you because you have chosen to answer the call of your soul. This can put a great deal of pressure on you, particularly if it is from someone close to you.

Many say friends and some family members rejected them when they began their spiritual path. This is ego to ego chatter and also fears from the other person radiating out. They fear you will change. That you won't be the same person any more and they won't enjoy the same influence over you. Sometimes there are religious reasons. Still your soul pushes you forward to overcome these outside opinions and to stay true to yourself.

As you begin your journey you feel happier, you gain a better attitude and most of all you become stronger within. You are now making and seeking positive changes in your life. Yet understand that your ego self has had its way for many lifetimes as I said. Stay alert. In staying alert and being aware of the ego in yourself and others, you will succeed on your journey toward a new you. Do not give in to self doubt. Whenever I experience self doubt I say a firm **no** to myself, then I tell it (the ego) to get out the back door. At the same time I have a sense that this is happening. You could try this. It may help you too.

The Importance of a Foundation

That is why it's so important to build a strong foundation. To replace some of those old worn out 'bricks' so your foundation becomes even stronger. It's only when you have a really strong foundation that you can recognize anything—a word, an action—that which is not of the Light and is from a lower vibration. With a stronger foundation you are able to hold onto and continue to build your higher truths.

So you can see once you recognize what's happening, your own self discipline can step in and kick that ego self out the back door. Here is an affirmation to help you when working with your ego self.

> **I control my ego**
> **I choose freedom of the Light**
> **I am free**

This is a very powerful affirmation. But it needs to be powerful for all those situations when your ego seeks to pull you back. You may like to copy this affirmation onto a card. Place it wherever you will see it continually. Allow the words to settle deep into your mind and to become a core belief. Affirmations are wonderful tools to help you to continue moving forward.

Your Past Lives

There have been times during your past lives when you have been crucified in various ways for speaking your truth. A higher truth. You may have been burnt at the stake, stoned to death or put to death by the guillotine because you used herbs to heal. Joan of Arc and many like her left us powerful legacies. Through the truth and her strong belief and faith Joan obtained victory. She is not forgotten all these years later. She must be very pleased.

But often a painful death experience remains in your soul memory and can create a 'block'. Because of this, speaking your truth and following a higher path in this life time can be stifled by an inner fear. The ego will grab onto those fears and use them to hold you back on a lower vibration. Remember the ego is lazy. It wants to stay in charge, the way it has done for many of your life times. The ego knows that higher awareness equals loss of lower power. So it will use many methods to hold you back. This is why it's so important to remain vigilant on your journey.

But let's look now at the scenarios I've just given you because it's important you completely understand this. If we go back to a time in your past life history when these events would've taken place, you would've been that outstanding shining Light in the time line shown to you in meditation. An example of goodness and Light to all. Others would look up to you because of this. However many would also hold negative attitudes and seek to influence others to their own way of thinking. You would be seen as a huge threat to their perceived power and control. Let's not forget that throughout history what man fears he either hides away or destroys. It has always been this way . . . til now. Those in power back then would seek to destroy you through death. They would do it in such a way as to make an example of you to be seen by all.

This can also play out on a smaller scale today in the office and business areas. As you become successful in any field, others can perceive you as a threat. However people are learning to transmute or integrate various negative energies now. Understand that these people are operating from their own fears. They are seeking to project that fear onto you, to belittle you and to end the perceived threat to them that they recognize in you.

Once you understand this you can move forward on your own path and actually become stronger because of the experience. You stay in your own power space by remembering the most powerful energy on Earth is at your disposal—the **Light.**

The Importance of Light Rays

Fear does not come from Light, issues of control do not come from Light, and negative thoughts do not come from Light. All of these responses come from darkness. Love cannot survive in darkness. Love can only shine as Light. So when love is placed with any dark emotion or situation the Light still shines forth into the darkness. Eventually the darkness will begin to fade and dissipate. That Light and that love is your *weapon* over darkness. Remember this.

If someone is speaking to you in a negative way simply visualize them in a ball of pink Light. Send them love via the Pink Ray. You don't have to stay in their space to do this. You can send the Ray of Love from anywhere and to anyone. This is because your intent, joined with your unconditional love goes out on the great Universal Web and connects with that person's higher self. It then filters down through their auric field to their conscious mind.

You will find they will stop being so negative. They may not understand why they suddenly feel more peaceful and calm. *You* know it's the power of love and intent. Use the Ray of Love wherever you feel you need to. Just sending this Ray will empower you immensely.

Your Focus

Understand clearly that whatever you focus your thoughts on you will draw to you to experience. Be aware that this includes your feelings as well. Verbally you could be saying, "I have financial abundance." But as you relax of an evening your mind may wander to a large bill which arrived in the mail. You begin thinking about how you're going to pay this bill. Wondering where you will get the money from. What could you go without? Everything was going ok and now you have this bill to pay. You say to yourself, "I just don't have the money!" Worse, you keep repeating those words. You notice a feeling of dread in the pit of your stomach. The entire feeling you are creating around the bill is one of lack! You are creating financial lack through your fear of not having the money to pay that bill. You are creating lack through your emotions.

So looking at what you've read so far about the ego self and how it works, you can now understand how you can easily fall backwards to old paradigms of fear and lack, and also how you can overcome anything in life. Self discipline is the key isn't it? Because that's what it takes to remind yourself to use the Light energy. Instead of drawing lack to you, use this affirmation—

> **I bless this bill.**
> **I pay this bill quickly and easily**
> **I enjoy financial abundance now.**

Light Quotient

You have probably heard of Light quotient. It means the amount of Light essence you hold within you. You gain your Light quotient in a number of ways. By turning the tide of your beliefs, expanding your higher understanding and therefore your DNA. Turning the tide of what you choose to experience. Choosing to live your truth. Every day living with Light and creating peace within and around you.

It's true that as you generate the vibration of more Light on Earth you will create what many now call a new Earth. This is how a new Earth will be created. Through positive, loving thought, true intent and peace and respect for all living things. In a place where Light abounds there is no place for power, greed and control. They cannot exist because these carry a negative energy field.

As you follow your own truth and your own inner knowing and integrity, your vibrational energy field increases. You are able to hold more Light and you increase your own Light quotient. The Light quotient is the level of Light and the vibration of that Light, that you can carry comfortably within your being. That level of Light quotient depends on your level of enlightenment. Your understanding of, and more importantly, living a higher truth. It's simple really. As Master Kuthumi says:

> **Spirituality is simple,
> it is man who chooses
> to make it so complicated.**

Spirituality is often complicated by man through ego and self importance. But spirituality *is* simple. The ancient truths remain. Follow your heart. Learn to listen to what your heart and soul is telling you. It's time to come out of the head and into the heart when deciding a course of action. Spirituality must be lived, not hidden away. It is not a religion; it *is* a way of life.

Each time you meditate you draw higher intentions into your mind. You fill yourself with Light and each time you meditate are able to hold a little more Light within. So your own Light energy builds. Master Kuthumi says,

"You will glow with Light and in time you will become Light."

Four years ago we had Become Light printed on our business cards, but no one really understood it's meaning back then. Now people are becoming more aware of the Ascended Masters and Arch Angels and other Light Beings who speak through various channels enabling man to understand so much more of the higher truths and the glorious essence they contain for all of us.

Chapter Five

The Great Release

We have covered the importance of releasing all hurts, resentments, jealousies and painful residues from previous experiences. You understand by releasing these emotions you become free. You take back your power. That power is no longer held by another in an on going victory over you. You see as long as you choose to continue to hold all that painful and angry emotion within the recesses of your mind you continue to give that issue victory because you still hold and feed the pain and hurt you hold deep within. The memories and the tightly held emotions stifle you and prevent you living your true potential. This is why weeding your garden is so important. It is a corner stone to your soul growth and therefore your personal growth.

Even if you've just found the courage to begin the great release, you will be feeling more freedom within as you release your inner demons of pain and fear.

You have now built a strong foundation. Continue to use the Soul Wash meditation whenever you feel the need to. It will help you greatly on your journey to freedom. However there is a key which you will need in order to step through to complete freedom. That key is the **Key of Forgiveness.** All the great Masters speak of forgiveness. Every person has the right to create their own fulfilment of happiness. Every person.

But until you reach that point of happiness, until you can forgive those people who caused you all the pain and grief, until you can do that you will not gain true happiness and freedom. You also need to forgive the most important person—**you**! Forgiveness means letting go of the pain and the memory. That doesn't mean it was ok, no. It means letting go.

Many hold a feeling of guilt within. We've discussed this. It is so important to forgive your self. The past is done. Why keep dragging it with you every day? It only weighs you down. How can you find your wings to fly when rocks of self guilt keep holding you down? Forgive and move forward.

One of the saddest things is when someone abuses a child. Abuse comes in many ways. Parents arguing for example. The child hears something they did mentioned. Instantly the child feels such guilt. They tell themselves they must be bad, it's their fault the parents they love so much are arguing. The child's immature mind is unable to rationalize or comprehend the situation in terms of reality and responsibility. So the child forms and holds onto self blame and guilt.

As the child grows when a situation arises it becomes easier and easier to continue to blame themselves. Often quite unreasonably. Anger begins to simmer within. The child turns from all aspects of authority and begins to lash out in order to try and quell the anger. Eventually the anger so tightly held within will create physical illness. The pain will continue until the experience is looked at honestly, understood and weeded out along with any issues of self blame.

This is an example, but it's one that many can relate to. It's also part of the law of cause and effect. Only this isn't karma as such. This is what the child has *unknowingly* done to themselves over many years. They have punished themselves over and over through being too ready to take the blame on board even if it really wasn't theirs to take. They chose to see that is was their fault at a very young age. Along with all this guilt came other baggage. Feelings of being unworthy of happiness. Being unworthy of love. Being unworthy of receiving kindness from others.

Women enter into abusive relationships because they harbor unworthy beliefs about themselves. They don't feel worthy of being loved. Men can feel these emotions too, and will often become loners, shunning friendships and society.

So you see how seeds planted in childhood can become such strong poisonous weeds. You *are* worthy of freedom. You might say that you can relate to this scenario. But how can you change? It begins with changing the inner patterns of your thinking. Remember the inner reflects the outer.

Change your thinking change your life

If you've been creating a wrong self image STOP! Right now, STOP. Get a diary. Set time aside to do the inner work. It's up to you. No one else can do this for you. We have given you the tools but it's up to you to do the work. For *you*. You create your reality. That new reality starts now!

Challenge those old issues and hurts. Challenge yourself. How do you really see yourself today? How is your 'weed' pulling going at this point of your journey?

The Bridge to Freedom

Time to start building a bridge. Begin with the fifth rung of the Cave Ladder. Do you remember the affirmation for this?

> **I have no lack in my life**
> **I only have unlimited possibilities**

But how can you truly believe this if you can't forgive yourself? If you don't love yourself even a little at this point? Way back I asked you to write down four things you *like* about yourself. Can you find that list? The four things you wrote are very important. These are the building blocks to your freedom. So what did you write? Read them, then read them again out loud. Now that you understand more about you, you may like to add more things you like about yourself to that list. The more the better. This is one list you want to give a lot of energy to. Read it over and over. Say "Yes, this *is* me." Focus on the good points about yourself and build on them. Stop giving energy to the past. I am going to give you a meditation from Master Kuthumi to help you forgive yourself and the past. To help you move on for good!

Angel of Light Meditation

Let's begin. Take the phone off the hook to ensure you won't be disturbed. Sit comfortably, feet flat on the floor.

Breathe in, completely filling your lungs, slowly breathe out through the mouth. Do this three times to align your subtle bodies and prepare.

Now breathe normally. You are feeling more peaceful and calm.

Visualize breathing in the Light energy. See it like a beautiful white mist. Breathe it in and see it filling your entire being. Keep breathing.

Now an Angel appears in front of you. Feel her wonderful loving energy. She is full of Light, serene and gentle. She reaches out and takes your hand. You feel safe and so loved. Take a moment to absorb her loving, gentle energy. Breathe

She takes you back to when you were a child, when you first began feeling hurt and blaming yourself. Don't see the details; just see yourself at that age.

The Angels soft wings gently enfold you. You feel safe now. The Angel tells you that you are filled with love, filled with Light. You are a beautiful loving child, cared for and loved greatly.

See the love, feel it, feel the Light emanating out around you and a renewed peace coming over you, a calmness as the old pain and blame is dissolved in the Angel's wings. She tells you that you have done nothing wrong.

Rest a while in the Angel's beautiful healing energy.

Now as you watch, see that child merge back to you. Integrate the child, the love and the renewed peace into your heart.

Breathe. Give thanks

Visualize bringing a beautiful clear pyramid over you.
See yourself inside the pyramid, safe, calm.
Now open your eyes.
You are now present once more.

Now read these words:
I am love, I am Light,
In love I forgive
In love all my pain is washed away

I forgive myself and those who caused me hurt and pain
I am Light
I am free
So be it and so it is.

You can use this meditation and verse to release and heal all the inner hurts that have held you captive for so long. Simply adjust the meditation to suit. Remember you don't need to relive the situation, just have the knowing of the event. You need to forgive yourself before you can truly forgive another.

You have awareness to perceive what is truth and what is not without judgement. To judge is wasted energy. Everything you need for this experience, this life is within you. Begin by noticing what you feel in any situation. How you feel about others. What is your intuition trying to show you? It's time to trust your inner feelings. Time to listen within. Time to value your own voice, your own opinions, not those of another outside of you.

This is part of freedom. Because freedom also means responsibility for yourself. Responsibility for your own words, your own actions, your own choices. Build a strong bridge.

Comparison to Yourself

How often have you compared yourself to some else? Now be honest. How often have you felt you fell 'short?' Every time you compare yourself to someone else you may feel a little limited. Why? The answer is because you secretly aspire to be like that person, or to have something they have. This could be a certain position or a job for example. People don't tend to compare themselves to someone they deem to be an equal. It's usually someone who *you* perceive is better than you, or someone who has accomplished something you wish to do.

This sets the scene for competitiveness. Let's look at a work scenario as an example. You see someone in another position that you perceive to be better than yours. You begin to compare. First the work load, what you think they'd be paid, then the status of the position. Without thinking you begin to compete with them. To strive to be like them. To have what they have. Some people will compete more than others. But this is not a good level to strive for. Why? Because you are seeing yourself as inferior right from the start. You have set a scene in play that you cannot win unless you enter into the ego self. Because to win you probably need to get nasty and devious. You begin listening and adding to gossip to enable you to get closer to your perceived goal. To be better—fast!

I ask you in this scenario are you respecting yourself? Are you loving yourself? Are you respecting someone else? No. No. No.

Everything you need is within. There is a great difference between wanting to better yourself for the right reasons and wanting to be in someone else's shoes. It is a very competitive world we all live in at present. But it is vital that you maintain faith in yourself and live in truth. Live in integrity and don't plant more 'weeds.'

A Project in Action

You gain great inner strength when you can forgive and love yourself—warts and all. In other words in spite of the past and perhaps your personality and short comings. We all have those you know. Everyone has something about themselves they don't like. Everyone. That may be the way they laugh, their hair, their nose, the fact they find it so hard to speak up. Lots of things. But you are a project in action. You're working on you and must accept that's what you look like, or that's just how you are. Accept *you*.

Change is easy when you have love and acceptance. That creates an easy road to growth. Once you achieve this a wonderful thing happens. You begin to really enter into your **soul power**. You do. You begin to see all those little things that really annoyed you before are just not so important after all. You begin to view things from a higher perspective.

You stop looking to others for love, for approval or acceptance. Because you no longer have a need to look outside of yourself for these. Everything you need is within you. You are now stronger and more confident. You can decide to be with someone and to share your life with them because you *choose* to, not because you feel you need to or you should. Whilst you would like their approval you don't *need* it. That's the difference.

This leads to a wonderfully happy and compatible relationship on all levels. Yet so much is written about love. Through romance novels some women develop the belief that you must have a relationship, you *must* have a partner. If you do you'll live happily ever after. So they learn this is the norm. I can tell you it's not. It is possible to live happily ever after, but because you *choose* to accept the other person. Their emotions, actions and their love. Not because you believe this is the *only* way you can be happy. Or that your happiness is dependant on another.

Love yourself first. Maintain balance within. Master Kuthumi has a request here to help you accept yourself and also to provide a great deal of soul growth for you. It is optional, but I can tell you it has been tested and the results were astounding. Not only was soul growth achieved, but huge emotional 'blocks' were cleared by each person allowing them to truly step into their soul power. It is simple, yet for some so difficult. We know that the more difficult it appears to us, the greater the learning.

Master Kuthumi requests you write a love letter—to yourself. Write it from your heart. Just as though you were writing to someone you know, someone you love dearly.

I can tell you this request was given on a webinar from Master Kuthumi. One woman, I'll call her Ann, I want to tell you about. Ann was in her fifties. She felt she had endured a difficult life. While she was young in the Second World War in Germany, she witnessed her mother and sister being raped and killed. Her beloved father was led into a large shed with others and was gassed. Ann witnessed other tragedies at this time. Yet Ann survived and went on to marry and move to another country. Years passed. Ann did her 'duty' in all aspects but could not give all of herself. Her emotional scars were very deep.

After many years of marriage, Ann knew she was in trouble with her relationship. She felt unfulfilled and her husband wasn't happy either. During the webinar Master Kuthumi gave the request to write a love letter. This had Ann thinking deeply about herself. Her experiences, her husband and her life. Ann wrote the most beautiful heartfelt, loving letter. She sent me a copy which moved me to tears. Writing that letter changed Ann's life. Finally, Ann was ready to let go of the horrific memories of her past and to move forward. To truly open her heart to true love after all these years. My reward came some weeks later when Ann wrote to me. She told me she felt reborn. After all these years she finally knows what love is. That is huge! Ann's life had changed so much; she now knew true happiness and an inner peace she had never experienced before.

There were other success stories of great magnitude which changed lives as well after students wrote their own love letter. But back to the present. How did you go? I truly hope you wrote the letter. You're worth it! As always you have choice. But I really hope you try. Honour yourself and all that you are. Keep this letter in your journal. It's a visual reminder of the new you!

I had a lady visit me a few days ago for a reading. She was a lovely lady in her sixties. She told me she felt angry. Angry that she hadn't discovered spirituality til now. She felt the knowledge had come too late in her life; she had missed so many years because of this. She saw there was so much more she could have achieved had she had the knowledge much sooner in her life.

I told her not to be angry. Be grateful! Grateful that now she did know, now she could experience her soul and find inner peace. All her years of precious experience had helped to mould her into the person she was today. When the student is ready, the teacher will appear. Her teacher had arrived in the form of her daughter who held the key to the door of her mother's soul. The important thing was that she hadn't left it too late.

This applies to many situations we all face in life. We have choices, always we have choice, but sometimes you just let it slide. You put it out of your mind and don't bother to even make a decision. It's less hassle to take an easy path. Sometimes months later the situation will be presented to you again. Chances are you will wish you had made a decision back then. But you didn't and though you have to make that decision now, things have changed in the meantime.

You know that you can't alter or change past events. You can simply learn. Spirit is always sending out messages and lessons for us. They do this in a number of ways.

The Planets Of Learning

One of the main ones is the transits of the planets in our Universe. Certain planets are at certain points when you take your first breath. This is called your Natal Chart in Astrology. It is a very important chart and contains a great deal of information about you as a person, and also your major points of learning in your current lifetime. It is really your own blueprint for your life. Each year at your birthday, a chart can be drawn up indicating your major lessons of experience in the coming year. This is called a Solar Return and takes twelve months from birthday to birthday to complete. Both of these charts can be obtained for you on our website <u>www.kuthumischool.com</u> under Astrology.

But spirit also sends us lessons in other ways. They constantly present doorways of opportunity. Sadly many of these are just not seen clearly so they pass a person by. You see we always have a choice whether to walk through a doorway of opportunity, or simply to stay put. Spirit cannot tell you exactly what to do in any situation. If you do go to a psychic and they say, "You should do this. You should do that," leave. Because they are not receiving guidance from a high source. They are listening to a lower entity and often 'lace' that knowledge with their own opinion! It's these types of psychics that give good ones a bad name and worse, create a negative understanding of a true psychic and their work. Very sad really I think.

You must decide yourself what path you want to experience in your life. Always there will be choice. Each path allows you a different experience to learn from. Spirit honours this and never tells you what to do. They suggest or show various paths of choice.

Words Are Powerful

You need to speak clearly for others to really understand your message. Let's look at the scenario of a discussion you're having on any subject. You talk, sometimes a little heatedly, but still talking. The conversation has ended. There are a number of points that you're not happy with. You wonder why the other person doesn't understand what you mean. Can't they see?

The answer is no, they can't. There are two reasons why not. One, because you haven't spoken clearly enough for them to understand your message, and two, because they haven't really listened. They have heard you, but haven't really listened.

It's interesting. Spirit gave me a powerful lesson on the importance of speaking clearly in a meditation circle over 32 years ago. I was told a 'Lynn' was going to be teaching classes in the future. Now there were two ladies named Lynn in the group. The teacher assumed it would be the other Lynn who seemed more advanced in her learning, so she gave her the message. Well, turned out it was to be the other Lynn— me! (I called myself Lyn back then.) The big lesson for me was always clarify exactly who the message is for. Be *very* clear when you ask Spirit for anything. I have never forgotten that lesson and I have passed it on to many students over the years. We need that same clarity when we converse with each other as well. Be very clear. Look the person who you're talking to in the eye. This demands that their focus be on you and you're words. Listening is important too. Sometimes you need to actually practise just listening clearly. You may be quite amazed.

Who's Perception?

Each person has a different perception of life, of love, of relationships. Each may see the world in an entirely different way. One may be prepared to work, is considerate and probably a little optimistic

71

too. Another person may have an attitude, thinks the world owes him. His ego self would probably be his friend. These are two very different examples, but the point is that each has a very different perspective on life.

It's not really the situation that matters you know. It's your attitude to that situation. How you perceive it? What do you choose to do about it? How do you choose to react to it?

Honour Yourself in All Things

You did the weeding already and remember this may well be an ongoing task. It takes time to look at and pull out those really big hurts and deeply held anger. So be kind to yourself. It doesn't matter how often or even when you have to do some more internal work. The important thing is that you keep up the maintenance.

You will now be very aware of any new weeds taking seed or sprouting. Be aware because they can be a bit sneaky. For instance, you may have words with a friend. Some of the things your friend tells you stick in your mind, (beware of the seeding process.) As you think them over later resentment begins to set in, (the seeding is done.) You may carry on the friendship but it will never quite be the same because you are carrying resentment over something they said to you. At this point you have a choice. You can do some inner work, or you can tell yourself it doesn't really matter and root out that seed of resentment. That seed won't go away until it's released and healed. You know this. You are the owner. Why would you want to keep it anyway to sit and grow into a giant weed?

Sadly, many people do. Many still go back to old paradigms of behaviour and simply try to ignore it. They push the words and the emotion down deep within them. Problem is when those words or similar are spoken to them again that seed begins to sprout. When other situations touch on that emotion the seed grows further into a weed and so on until before you know it, you have a huge very painful weed. The weed's food is your own energy. It is you who keeps that weed alive, who allows it to grow. Yes, you!

Trust can be a big weed as well. There are many types of weeds. Remember we learn from what we create. What we choose to experience. Sure someone helped you feel resentful or mistrusting but it's *you* who chooses how you're going to deal with those emotions and therefore, your reactions.

So here you are. A soul with some big emotional weeds to clear. Your soul family member has played their part in the creation of that experience, however painful. There are many reasons why we choose various experiences but *all* are for learning and soul growth. You may have become very angry with that person. Yet that person may be very close to you in spirit—on a soul level. They help you to experience, to learn with unconditional love, knowing you may never speak to them again in this life time. Understand from a higher perspective they love you very much. The experience is knowledge. How you react is soul growth. Do the inner work. Honour yourself and let it all go.

You may feel silly writing that love letter to yourself. I can tell you that nothing Master Kuthumi asks you to do is silly. It gave you strength. It showed you self love. It gave you a different perspective of yourself. That strength is probably needed now because it takes courage to look deep within and do this work. You are now able to have more forgiveness in your heart for yourself and for others.

Forgiveness is the key in this process. I hope now that you have more higher knowledge, you will also be more aware of not allowing seeds to germinate and sprout on your emotional body. It does require constant vigilance, but it's worth it. *You* are worth it!

Finding your own Gold Nugget

I think we've all experienced this. At times you just ignored what you wanted to do and simply gave in to someone else's thinking and wants. "If I do that they'll like me." *Like me* are the over riding words here. Some put others first to a ridiculous point and just accept anything that's left for themselves. Money, time, food, love. They put themselves last when they should be putting themselves first. Sound familiar? Now I'm not talking about being selfish and uncaring, all must be in balance but learning to say no can be very hard to do.

All too often people pleasers are seen to appear timid, easy going and they often allow themselves to be taken advantage of. Strong people see them as a push over. Sometimes so much so they actually border on abusing an easy going person because they don't give them a choice. They either don't think about what the other person really wants, or just decide to bully the person into doing what they want. The quieter person rarely objects. They hold their hurt and anger within, trying not to let their emotions show. There may have been many times when they tried to speak up and object. Sadly they got ridiculed and shouted down, so they have learnt over time to say nothing. Sad, but true.

I don't think the quieter person really does just want to submit all the time. I think they don't really respect or love themselves enough. They have a low self esteem because of this and often just feel unworthy. But you know, each one is a gorgeous gold nugget underneath all that. However they don't see themselves this way and carry a lot of inner anger. Overtime that anger they try so hard to hide, will manifest as a physical disease as I've already said.

It's good to consider others but don't lose yourself in the process. As a soul your birthright allows you to have limitless prosperity, hope and happiness on all levels. This is part of the Law of Creation. You may ask, "Well, where is it?" Where indeed. It hasn't moved away or left you. You have through your conscious beliefs. The ones you created for yourself. You dislike and punish yourself, chastise yourself often yet expect to receive limitless abundance and happiness for yourself. What is this saying to the Universe?

You can turn this around you know. Yes you can. Recognition is 80%. Remember the love letter? It was a new beginning. Don't leave it too late. You create your life. You also create physically, emotionally and mentally to the Universe in the Now, which in turn creates your future. The Universe listens to creations of a loving intent. A correct intent. They will only answer loving intent.

So try to pause for a moment when a sub-conscious 'button' is pushed. Ask, "Is this my stuff or theirs?" Do it often. It will soon become a habit. That pause is enough to lift you to a higher plane of truth so you can cope with any situation instead of getting bogged down in emotional 'sludge.' This really works believe me.

Instant Karma exists Now

Things are changing on Earth. We now have instant karma. Cause and effect. We used to have to work out our karma over various lifetimes. This was a long process as you can imagine. We lived in a lower three dimensional energy then. Everything was a heavier energy. It often took two or three lifetimes to learn one lesson! Oh how slow that seems to us now. Yet it really wasn't that long ago. As recent as around 1910. Everything took time but we had plenty of time back then.

But now in 2013 time has really sped up. Have you noticed? We no longer have the time to spend many lifetimes on karma and learning our lessons in order to gain higher wisdom. So the Universe has now moved us to instant karma. This means if I do something to deliberately hurt you, you don't need to be the one who 'pays' me back. Nor does that payback have to be in a similar way as my hurt to you. No. Now someone else can pay me back and it can be instantly, certainly within two or three days. So—instant karma. Cause and effect.

What have you caused and what is the effect of that on someone else? Sadly some people blame everything on karma. You hear it everywhere, "Oh, it must be karma." Why? Why must it? There are many reasons and not necessarily karmic.

A Reflection on Your Creation

Let's look at another. That friend or workmate who's really annoying you. Could it be that they are actually mirroring for you? Could it be they are showing you a side of you in some way? Maybe a reaction, a character trait, or simply a strong flavour of your personality. Usually when someone is mirroring you, you react quite harshly and often with aggressive anger. This is a situation which calls you to be totally honest with yourself. Look deep within because often it's a facet of yourself you don't want to acknowledge readily. But if you want to advance on your path of enlightenment you need to look carefully and be honest with yourself. Think of the Law of Creation. What are you creating? What is the person's 'reflection of behaviour' showing you? This is certainly something to consider when you're faced with this type of feeling and situation.

Create a Life You Love

You need to realize you can create a world you love, including you and the part you play. Everyone plays a part. Everyone experiences good and not so good. We all have, not just in this lifetime, but in previous lifetimes as well. It's called polarity. You need to experience good and bad because if you didn't how could you recognize one from the other? You couldn't because you didn't have the experience to know which was better or worse. So here you are and I'm saying to create a world you love because it's time to do so. Mankind has experienced great polarity and now we are being asked to take off our armour, to come back to soul remembrance, to love and feel happiness and joy. To acknowledge you have the power to create what you want.

For years so many spirit guides and Beings of Light have told us repeatedly of the power of our thoughts. At first we couldn't comprehend. Many wondered how could we do that? It sounded so difficult as we would have to monitor every thought. Now, here we are some fifty years later and the message is even more relevant today. But today you have a greater understanding of why you need to watch your thoughts. Mankind has a greater understanding of Soul, of the Universe, and how the two are intertwined. You understand energy and how it works. What you give out in thought or deed, you will receive back for better or for worse. So you create. You may say," Oh but so and so said that to me. How could I create that?" It is true that you cannot control what another says or does to you. However you can and do create your own reaction—your response. Here lies the key to your creation. What do you choose to do? How do you choose to react?

Do you choose to take it on board and fight back? Become angry and retaliate or feel hurt and resentful. How do you choose to react? You can speak your truth, quietly and clearly. You can listen while asking yourself, "Is this their stuff or mine?" You *do* have the power over what you choose to create—every day! Think about what you want. What sort of lifestyle do you want? You could write in your dairy some ideas of what you want in your life today?

Why not try, just for the next seven days, to write in your dairy each night five things you are grateful for that day, and five things you could've reacted to in a better way. At the end of the seven days read back over your notes. Think about how much more aware of your reactions you are now. Think how you now look at situations.

Interesting isn't it? Continue writing if you wish. Remember . . . you're worth it!

Chapter Six

You Are the Creator

You are on a planet of choice. You know that. Every minute, yes every minute of every waking day you use that choice. You can choose from having a drink of water, opening a draw, deciding about your job, a friend or thinking about something you heard on the news. You are making choices. You decide what to eat, what to wear, are you too hot or cold? Lots of choices from everyday events to larger decisions.

You see how you create your daily reality and also your future. Each choice carries a responsibility for what you create. You are responsible for what you create by your thoughts, actions and words. You are a very powerful being. Did you ever think of yourself as powerful—a universal powerful being? Well you are. Yes indeed. But let's take this even further. If you are responsible for what you create in your own world and in your future, what about the larger world and the planet?

You are making decisions and experiencing various emotions so imagine for a moment that emotion, whether it be anger, anxiety or happiness, but just imagine that emotion multiplied by 6 ½ billion times! Can you further imagine the power of that energy around the planet? Just think of the power of that much anger or anxiety or worry—which is real! We have this on the planet right now. Can you imagine? Can you begin to see what a thick fog of negative energy millions of people have built around the planet over hundreds of years? Mankind has created this. Many individual's thoughts and emotional energy has amassed to form an energy like a dark fog around our planet.

The Importance of Intent

So you begin to see how far reaching and how powerful intent is. Weren't we just talking about your thoughts, your actions and emotions? Let me tell you your intent followed your first thought— whatever that was. It was your choice and then your intent carried it forward to an action. You can take this example right down to a simple cup of tea. So emotion could be called thought in action. It *is* powerful.

Man has not yet fully understood this because he refuses to take full responsibility for his thoughts and actions. So the realization of the available power of what he creates has not been fully understood.

Now let's come back to you personally. Think for a moment of what you have created around you. Most of it will be good. But there may be some things which haven't quite worked out the way you thought they would. You have a choice—there's that word again. But you do. You can mope around, moan and groan and feel sorry for yourself because your decision didn't quite work out as well as you thought it would. You can go into victim mode and enter the cave. Or, you can think about what it would take to make the situation better. What would that take? What is it you need to stop doing, to take away or change?

The first step is you need to decide *exactly* what you want to create. The second step is to decide how you're going to *achieve* it. A friend of mine, Adam, found that by changing his thought and his intent—and taking that through to action provided him with some great results in his work. Adam's energy has also changed without him realizing it. He has opened up and gained more confidence. Although Adam knows he may not be successful every time, he doesn't mind. Because he's now looking at the bigger picture of his work and his life.

When you are walking and you stub your toe you don't sit down; feel sorry for yourself and just stop. No you pause, acknowledge you hurt your toe, perhaps give it a rub, and keep moving forward. People who do this become *winners*. They keep moving forward. Keep focused. Keep looking at the bigger picture of what they want to achieve through that change. They make that change happen.

Fertilize Your Future

How could you do this and what does fertilize mean? It's a metaphor of course. Just as you weeded your garden you now need to fill your emotional body with positive energy. But life isn't always positive is it? Everyone has bad days. And we all know what it's like when someone else ruins our day by their anger or actions. So what's the answer? It all comes down to intent—*your* intent and the choices you make. However you choose to react will decide the outcome of the situation and also what energy you release out into the planet's atmosphere along with 6 ½ billion others.

So what do you think you'll choose? You know all about the cave. I think now you're quite familiar with cave behaviour and more importantly, more aware of the crucial time of *entering* the cave. Remember that 80% is recognition. That is crucial. The remaining 20% however is everything because you have to decide what you will do and how you will react. Do you see?

Four Important Steps to Success

So if you want to create your future and fertilize it how can you do that? Here are the four important steps to success. You can use these simple steps in various situations as the basic four steps will still apply.

One:

Decide on what it is you **want** to create in your life. Make it realistic, not something you know is very difficult or impossible to achieve. By choosing something you know is very difficult to actually achieve you are self sabotaging. If you do this, you need to do more weeding.

Two:

Decide **how** you will achieve your goal. How will you create it? Break your goal down to easy to achieve steps. Each step takes you closer to achieving your goal and making it a reality—your reality. Write down each step of what you need to do to reach your goal.

Three:

Focus, **focus**, focus. Keep visualising your creation. See it in your mind's eye. Feel it. See yourself at your goal—success!

Four:

Keep repeating and **believe** this affirmation—

> **I achieve (state your goal) now,
> easily and with ease. I am
> blessed by this process.**

These are your four steps to success! You fertilize a step each time you visualize yourself successfully living your goal. Knowing and *believing* you *can* achieve your goal.

Remember the CAN DO (Your Name) button? How this empowers you and allows you to 'pretend' until you make it. This encourages your mind to believe in you as well. Your CAN DO button reaffirms this and accepts it as truth—your truth. Added to this you now have intent. Wonderful glorious intent to help you to achieve your goal. Your intent carries your goal through to positive action and confidence. The CAN DO button helps to fertilize your action as well. Here is another simple affirmation to help you achieve your desire. Each morning as you comb your hair in front of the mirror, look your self in the eye and say—

> **I'm a Winner!**
> **I'm a Winner!**

Do this every morning. You'll soon feel a difference in yourself. Because you **are** a winner and your CAN DO button is right there with you.

Such is life. You may find you have a task to do which you don't really want to do. Your ego self may begin telling you in your mind, "You know you don't have to. Why not just sit down and leave it." Warning! Red light! Danger! Cave in front of you. Watch out!

Instead force yourself to smile. Your body will begin to release the happy hormone Serotonin. Remind yourself with this affirmation

> **I can do it, I can do it.**
> **I don't have problems,**
> **I only have positive results in my life!**

Smile again. Feel better? Gather up your Can Do button and get to it. Remember this button is your help buddy.

There are two words you need to permanently remove from your vocabulary. **I Can't.** If you accidently catch yourself saying these words, catch it and say delete! Instead if saying I can't, say **Can Do (Your Name)**!

Change your words, change your intent and you change your life! Aristotle said, "What you said that you shall find." He should have added the word think as well, what you think you will find.

You grow old because you expect to. You accept this as your truth and so it is and shall be. You accept your body will wear down. You'll get illness, aches and pains as you grow old—so it is so. It is your truth. *You* believe it to be so. What you think you will create for yourself.

Psychological studies have proven time and time again the basic reason a person will be successful is because *he expects to succeed*! It has become his truth. He *believes* it to be so.

Remember Muhammad Ali the boxer? Whenever he was interviewed he never used the words *if* or *maybe*. He always said "When I win" or "I will win." These words were his belief, his truth and they became his reality. He expected nothing less than to win his boxing matches and to achieve success. He did just that as history has shown.

Your expectations will and do shape your life. Whatever your expectations are you will attract those expectations to you. If you expect the worst to happen—it will. When you expect something to happen it is already firmly planted in your mental body via your thoughts. That is the message you are sending out to the Universe. There is a Kahuna saying—

> **Energy goes where
> attention flows**

As I said, your self confidence is built engaging in positive expectations. But there's another matter to consider. Some people cling to past events in their lives through possessions including old letters and other trivia. I'm not saying don't have any of these, but please keep them in perspective. Don't focus your life on them. They are memories, often beautiful memories. You need to live in the present. To focus on your goals and successes. You may want to make a Wish Board to help you with achieving your goals. This can be for a single present goal you want to achieve, or a multiple set of goals for the coming year.

Make Your Own Wish Board

First you need to focus not only on what it is you wish to achieve, but also on *you* as well. So often people focus on a new car, lots of money, a trip ect. But what about you? Where will you be? Will you be happy, content? There is also another aspect to remember to portray on your wish board—your emotions. So in making your wish board you need to consider your inner world, (emotions) and your outer world, (goals.) Take time with considering what you really are wishing to accomplish or to have. Remember what you focus on, you create. Make it your truth. It's important to stay focused. Don't change your mind in the coming days or weeks.

So once you know your goal gather your supplies. First a large piece of cardboard. You can choose a coloured one to make it more personal if you wish. All colours carry an energetic pattern. For example, red is action, green is healing, blue is calming, pink is love, purple is spiritual, white encompasses all colours.

Next you'll need some magazines. Ones with lots of pictures. With sharp scissors, cut out the pictures relating to your goal. For example, if another home was your goal then you would cut out a picture of a similar looking home to the one you want and a similar size of home. Is there a front fence? Are there trees around the new home you want? You would also want to write on your board how many bed rooms, how many offices and living rooms? You could use a coloured pen for this if you wanted to. Are the rooms big or small? Does it have a garage? This is just an example, but it gives you an idea of how to create your own Wish Board. Details are important.

Of course you can decorate the board with other things pertaining to your goal. For instance, you can cut out and glue onto your Wish Board pictures of money, a photo of you smiling and happy, (emotions) and other things you would like to achieve as well. Like success in study, or public speaking to name a few. Your Wish Board is whatever you want to achieve within reason. So know what you can comfortably achieve with your goals.

Finally tape your completed Wish Board to a wall or door where you will see it every day. As you look at it frequently you reaffirm your goals and wishes to your sub conscious mind and to the Universe.

Affirmation:

> **I replace the words "I can't"**
> **with "I should."**

Well, we've covered quite a lot so far. Each subject is a stepping stone to a new you and a new life. Don't leave it too late to honour yourself. Create a life you love. Fertilize your future with the Wish Board and the Can Do button. If you are having an inner battle with your self you need to sit quietly, go within and find that 'weed'. Ask yourself, "Is this issue my stuff, or their stuff?" If it is your stuff then deal with it. Own up to it. Then release it. If it's not yours then there's no point in holding onto it and worrying over it. Let it go.

When we are children we often hear things we don't understand. We can't really. We haven't yet developed the mental capacity to understand. So we formulate mind pictures. Some do this more than others. But we do tend make 2 + 2 = 5. In other words we misunderstand.

This happens a lot as adults too. We don't hear correctly or we actually hear the words differently. We imagine a different scenario. This happens in personal relationships as well. Often nothing is said. The misinterpretation isn't dealt with. The misunderstanding grows and grows. The couple withdraw and move apart emotionally. Time goes on. They move further apart. Before you know it they can't remember where it all began.

It Began with the Word

Misinterpretation of the word. So you see it is important to clearly understand, to listen, and to say what you mean. When you ask Spirit something you need to be very clear. Otherwise Spirit may answer you about something else they thought you asked and you receive the wrong message. This wasn't what you were expecting.

If you aren't sure what you want, Spirit won't answer you. I find this a lot with women. Since women tend to ask me more about relationship issues I refer to women here. They tell me they want a relationship. 'When will I have one?" they ask me. Later in the same conversation they relay how they love their freedom, making their own decisions and having their own 'space.' Now really, if you were listening to this what would you think? I can tell you Spirit think this lady isn't sure what she wants. So they do nothing. You must know what you *really* want.

We also need to learn not to take things personally. I am a very sensitive person and I get hurt easily so this is a huge lesson for me. I continually have to remind myself that a lot of intuitive people are sensitive. They don't like the energy of angry words or aggression. It grates on their Soul Light you see. We are all responsible for how we see and hear the world. We project what we perceive and what we feel. We can blame no one else. We must take responsibility for how we perceive things. It *is* our choice.

So let me ask you now how do you perceive yourself? Has your perception changed since you began reading this book? What are you projecting to the world? You know you are not your hair, your clothes or your figure. You are a beautiful soul behind all that. You need to remind yourself of that often.

Our world is changing. Our perception of our role is also changing. It used to be women to stay at home and the men went to work to earn the money for the food and home. Men were looked on as responsible for this, even superior. Now it's all changing. Women are working in top executive roles. This is not to say women are better. The scales are being balanced which is great from a soul level. Men now take a more active role with raising their children. They accept they have emotions and that it's ok to cry. So today there is the acceptance and the blending of both genders within.

You are reconciling the left and right brain. This is important as our planet moves further through the Photon Belt energy and enters the Galactic Equator. Many are now 'waking up' and realizing there is so much more than we can physically see. People are realizing its ok to own your feelings.

I think a great deal of this comes from inner confidence. How do you see yourself? I asked you this before. It's important because your perception of you is everything. How you communicate and how you respond to others is important. How you interpret what others say. Hopefully at this point, you *do* feel more confident in yourself. You understand more and are so much more aware. You see yourself as worthy of having all your dreams fulfilled. I ask you on a scale of 1-10 how much do you believe you are worthy of having your dreams fulfilled?

This scale factor is proof of how much confidence you have in yourself. How much you believe in yourself. There is a saying by Rainier Maria Rilke;

'Being an artist means not numbering or counting, but ripening like a tree which doesn't force its sap and stands confidently in the storms of spring, not afraid that summer may come. It does come, it always comes.'

When you feel really stuck and unsure I have one sentence which always helps me. It's very simple yet very effective. Say to yourself, "I surround myself in God's Light." That's it. Just one powerful sentence.

Try to visualize Light all around you, then breathe it in. In a couple of minutes, once the Light energy filters through to your physical body you will feel so much better and calmer.

Call the Light Brigade

There is another wonderful spiritual tool to help you when you just can't seem to solve a particular problem. When no answer is coming to your mind and the more you try for an answer the more elusive it seems to be and your head feels thick and heavy why not go visiting the higher realms. This is where I find my answers. I open myself to ask, to listen quietly, and to observe everything I'm shown from my higher self and from the Masters. I'm usually shown a different point of view to my own. I receive a Divine answer because my higher self is in full reception. I feel at peace so I let go of my worry and anxiety.

This is the process of let go and let God. Your higher self is a direct link to Divine Intelligence. How can you go wrong? Because this is so important and such a great help Master Kuthumi has asked me to take you through the process step by step. It's quite easy really. The main thing is to be open and to completely relax yourself on all levels. By that I mean not just the physical but your mental and emotional bodies as well. So try not to think, just feel. Don't analyse til later—if you must. Sometimes you feel like crying simply because of the incredible energy. Remaining calm is essential to this process. So get a comfortable chair and remember to turn off the phone as you don't want to be disturbed. Ask one question at a time. Find your quiet comfortable spot and we'll begin.

Communicating With Your Higher Self Meditation

Take a big deep breath in through your nose. Really fill up your lungs.

Slowly let it out through your mouth. Do this three times, and then gently focus on relaxing the physical body.

Relax the muscles in your legs, your torso, your arms and hands, your shoulders and neck, your facial muscles. Allow any remaining thoughts to float away—further and further away like autumn leaves.

Now you are feeling relaxed and peaceful.

Focus on a ball of white Light above you. See yourself gently rising to that ball of Light. When you reach the Light you will feel even more peaceful.

Gently and quietly ask your angel or guide to be with you. Feel them and be aware of their presence.

Now quietly ask in your mind your question concerning your problem or dilemma.

Relax and be open to feeling, seeing, hearing.

Go with what you first feel, see or hear. This is your higher self communicating with you. Trust. You must be relaxed to receive higher communication.

When you feel you have the process is complete, thank your angels and guides and slowly return to awareness, opening your eyes when you are ready.

Once you've done this exercise a few times the answers get longer, believe me.

You *will* be shown your answer. It is quite likely very different from what you thought or wanted to do. But remember this answer is from God through your higher self. It's a higher point of view. Your own thoughts didn't feel right to you or you wouldn't be seeking a better solution. Your higher self always seeks a higher path and soothes your soul. After a while you will understand that by really listening to your own higher self your life will be so much better in every way.

There are times when you continue to give your attention to another's needs and ignore your own. It is likely that sooner or later you will sabotage what you give and the way you give. You may withdraw, feel resentful or alienated and become desperately out of balance. Your attention spreads to so many things outside of you. It's very easy to slip into old mode behaviour and finds yourself back in the cave.

We are all living in very crucial times on Earth. You are aware of the cave. You can also recognize when someone else has entered the cave. But you are still in the process of turning those old habits around. You need to stay vigilant. There are times when we hold onto negative responses from another in our mind. Other times when we've had a bad day, and times when we just feel down. This little exercise is great and it may just help you in those times of need when you need a cleanse of your all your bodies.

The Duster Exercise

Make a day and time to give yourself ten minutes of quiet time with no interruptions.

Do the 3 breath exercise as before.

Gently enter your freedom space—not quite in your meditative state, about half way.

Don't connect to thoughts or happenings of the day. Just be still.

Now visualize a white feather duster. The feathers are long and lush. This is a magnificent full feathered duster with a long handle. Take time creating your duster.

Say to yourself, "I'm ready to clean out the rubbish holding me down."

What do you see, what do you hear, and what do you feel? What are you being shown by your higher self?

Dust the rubbish out of you. Understand in this higher state things don't have to be logical or have a meaning. Dust away that negative feeling from things going wrong, dust away any negative thoughts, dust away that gossip you heard, etc. If nothing comes repeat the words again.

When you feel you're finished, just rest a moment in the pure energy of Spirit and allow the energy to replenish every cell in your body. Now gently open your eyes.

This is a good exercise to do at least once a week to keep your auric field clear. This will also clear your mental and emotional bodies. You'll feel so much better and able to cope with life. You see as you raise your vibration of energy you become more sensitive to harsh environments and words. So if someone has been nasty to you clean out the rubbish with The Duster exercise. Keep your soul space clean by doing the house keeping. Aren't you worth it? Now since I've mentioned soul I'd like to talk about another important point in your development. This one is huge on your path of higher awareness.

Own Your Feelings

We've just talked about some of this. What to do when we're faced with difficult situations from others. I've just given you an exercise to clear the emotional and mental bodies. But what happens if a feeling of resentment or anger sticks in our mind like glue? What can you do? Life's not perfect—yet. The answer is *you own the feeling*.

I know you're often told to move it on but sometimes you just have to own it and admit to it. Say, "I'm mad because . . . . I feel angry because . . . . You know, there's always a 'because'. Because you need to understand the '*why*'. You need to tell yourself why. Your ego self will tell you no, let it go, it doesn't really matter. Look, just tuck it down (solar plexus) and you'll be fine. It's ok to feel mad if you want to. Recognize this as the ego. Remember it seeks to pull you back to old behaviour. It will use pain, fear, and rage as companions to your present anger and resentment.

So you need to know what the 'because' is. Own it. Don't try to resist it. You've done that in past life times. When you own it, you've told yourself *why* you feel angry. You see in the bigger picture of things it's not really that important. It's not such a big deal that will hold you back from your soul development. You've had an experience. It made you angry, resentful, maybe feeling hurt as well. Why would you want to keep those feelings tucked away inside of you to fester and chain you in darkness? Your angry. Own it. It's ok.

We're all on Earth to experience, to learn and to grow. To expand our beautiful souls of Light. How important will that anger or resentment be in your future? *What are you going to feed your soul?*

It's time to come out of your head and into your heart. Place that confused or negative feeling into your heart space and watch it dissolve. Give it to the Light through the love and compassion in your heart. Now give yourself a mind-heart hug. That's a special hug with higher energy where you feel safe, protected and loved. When you feel secure with no fear, it's easy to transmute any anger and just let it go.

Chapter Seven

Polarity of Creation

Throughout this book you have learnt to let go of crippling behaviour and negative habits. You can see that these no longer hold a place in your life because you have grown beyond those old patterns of behaviour. You are moving forward on your soul path. You can see it's not so difficult after all to change your behaviour patterns which just held you back. You *Can Do* it. What you once thought as impossible and too difficult, you now know you *can* do it—if you choose to.

On your soul path you will continue to undergo periods of change which provide opportunities for new growth. You will be like the snake that continually needs to shed it's skin as it outgrows the old one. Never fear this for there is nothing to fear. This book has already given you so many tools to deal with various situations. So why fear at all? It really is just a matter of letting go of old behaviour and thinking patterns and *allowing* yourself to 'shed your skin' and move on to the new you. A better and happier you.

At this point you begin to trust. This projects you higher to another level. It's a new learning now. You can begin to let go of trying to work everything out in the physical. You can trust that everything will just work out as it's meant to in the Divine scheme of things.

What you are doing now is like a self renovation. You are renovating the 'old' you. No one else can do this. Only you. You get to choose. Each little step—you choose. Each little hurt you let go of because you choose to. Each old behaviour pattern you change, you choose to do so. It is you alone who decides how you will change and to what level. You have to climb the ladder out of the cave. No one can do it for you. This is polarity in action!

You are done with experiencing old hurts, thoughts, emotions and behaviour patterns. But know also that this experience has provided you with growth and knowledge. But you decided it's now time to change. How much you change is up to you. It may be a little change, a series of little steps, or a big change.

There's no right or wrong, only experience. That's why it's so important to look at your past including your perceived mistakes. Look at these as an experience. But always try to learn from them. Master Kuthumi is always saying, "There are no mistakes. There is only learning." It's true when you think about it.

If you choose not to learn something important for your soul growth the Universe will just keep presenting you with the experience again and again, perhaps dressed differently each time, but still the same thing until you decide enough and you finally get it. Polarity in action is your choice. From the negative to the positive. But how could you recognize the positive if you never experienced the negative? You would have nothing to gauge what positive was would you?

Look to Positive People

Positive people allow themselves the right to experience a vast range of emotions from despair, anger and grief, to joy, excitement, and happiness. They allow themselves the right to experience. And positive people will often be drawn to use their limitations to their advantage and to help others in various ways.

They draw on their own experience and emotions for empathy with others. They understand how another feels so they become the most effective teachers of soul.

Still others think the answers to life are always outside of themselves. Or they keep waiting for an angelic being to cross their path and save them with a magical wand. Of course that won't happen so they just keep waiting, sabotaging their own growth.

You see, it's all about *you* taking responsibility for you. You aren't responsible for anyone else's words, actions, behaviour or choices. You are only responsible for your own. You're also responsible for how you choose to interpret another's behaviour. What your reaction will be. That's the key to everything really. *How* you choose to react. So learn to use your limitations to your own benefit. Once you understand this you can become an ambassador for Spirit. How good is that?

Build New Confidence

Most people are unable to feel confident in themselves until they have built a solid foundation through realizing they can be self sufficient. This doesn't mean acting as though you are perfect or above everyone else. It does mean you are quite capable of standing on your own two feet and being comfortable with who you are.

Yet many people give their power away so freely by thinking someone else is smarter or better than them. So the pattern develops of looking to others for their welfare and happiness. They depend on someone else outside of them. They tend to want that other person to have a magic wand to make everything better, to make those difficult decisions and tell them what to do when they should be taking the responsibility for themselves and their own decisions. But then that doesn't leave any one else to blame when things don't quite work out as planned does it?

If this is you then you need to decide if it's time to change. Often these patterns began in childhood or through the teenage years. You may have been put down often or made to feel not good enough. There are a number of reasons why. But the important thing is to ask yourself if you're ready to change. Once you recognize a behavioural pattern needs to change you can begin. Sometimes the really hard part is just admitting it to yourself. After all that's the first step. But once you do you can begin step by step to take control of your own decisions and your own life.

When you were a baby you only cared about you and your own welfare. You were totally dependant on what others could do for you. You required warmth, food and love. Even as babies some need more attention than others. But you quickly learnt if you cried someone came running. You then got held, fed, a nappy change. You learnt quickly the art of manipulation to survive at a very young age.

Sometimes a baby cries for fun or for attention. When a baby does this we understand. However, as an adult this type of behaviour becomes crippling to ones growth. The greatest gift any parent can give a child is self confidence. To learn to be responsible for themselves, their own decisions and actions. Sure they may fall along the way but a loving parent is always around to listen and to help the child learn and grow into a well adjusted adult through positive experiences and taking responsibility for choices made.

Recognition of Your Own Worth

Recognizing your own self worth is crucial to building self confidence. Throughout this book you've discovered a lot of steps to help you reach this point and to help you see yourself in a different light. I'm talking about acceptance of your accomplishments and talents. I'm talking about self acceptance—warts and all including accepting your past and your mistakes. Self acceptance of <u>all</u> of you. This has nothing to do with ego. It has everything to do with realizing you *are* unique. You are a beautiful soul living a human experience.

There are many wonderful and talented people who have tremendously low self esteem. Artists come to mind. On the surface they have everything. Money, clothes, magnificent mansions to live in and a glitzy lifestyle. They write fantastic music. Others make thousands of people laugh out loud. Then, with often no warning, they take an overdose of drugs and kill themselves. Others attempt to drown themselves in alcohol. You wonder why. The world looks at what the artists have presented to them. The glitzy lifestyle, the confidence, the laughing face and the wonderful talent.

But it's just that isn't it? It's what they choose to present to everyone. That's what we see. Yet often behind all the glitz and big smiles is a tragic story of low self esteem, little self confidence and tremendous self criticism. It's all hidden behind a smiling mask.

One of the main factors in low self esteem is to look at how your parents saw themselves. Because they were your first role model, your first teacher of life. Many model themselves on their parents behaviour until, usually as adults, they begin to see themselves as an individual.

Sometimes they don't like what they see. But they don't have to stay that way. Change is very possible. There are many facets of creating change throughout this book. You *Can Do* it!

> **You experience the bad days so you can really appreciate the good ones.**

That's the core really. The Polarity of Creation. The good, the bad, and the not so good. Understand this. Know that nothing remains stagnant in the Universe, even you. Any behaviour pattern can be changed—if you *want* to change it. If you don't like the way you react to a particular situation—change it. Interestingly when you begin to look at these issues it's because they are now outdated, they're past their use by date in behaviour patterns. You have outgrown them, so you begin to not feel happy and to want to change your own patterns for the better. Isn't that great? It's called awareness. So give yourself a huge pat on the back. Yey!

Here's another great affirmation to help you.

> **There are great benefits for me through this change and this is positive change for me.**

You must motivate the change you wish to make within yourself. Don't always rely on other people and don't compare yourself to anyone else. It's time to develop positive motivation. During your period of inner change try not to use the words—bad, I can't and wrong. Instead try to use the words—wise, I can, it's good.

Do not use words to judge yourself. You will change as your awareness changes. Any decision you make is based on your level of awareness and your own perception. *Perception is reaction.*

What do you choose? It is you and no one else who chooses. Own it. Take responsibility. That's your first step to take control of you and your life. This is a big part of why you incarnated to Earth. To experience polarity in everything. To experience free will—choice. So look on everything in your life as experience. It is you who reaps the rewards or suffers the consequences depending on how you react to *any* situation.

Ask yourself—how much do I want this? How great do I see my need to change? Ask. Because to create permanent change you must be 100% convinced that it is in *your* best interests to do so! Affirmations are a great help to achieve positive results and a firm resolve. For example if you desire something, no matter how small that level of desire is, you will not give it up. There is another way which helps a lot too.

Look Through the Eyes of your Heart

It's going within and connecting to your heart. Seeing yourself through the eyes of your heart. This is just magical and it can be a great help when you feel 'stuck.' The previous meditations given in this book will show you how to achieve this.

Don't give your past power. It's already been done. You've already experienced it. It's completed. Your past can only hurt you if you allow it to, if you keep feeding it thoughts and emotions. Let it go. If your past still keeps coming up, stop! Tell yourself again as many times as necessary—"It's done. It's behind me. I give it no energy." Remind yourself as often as you need to. Get out your abundance ladder and do the steps. You know this is *positive creation*. You are taking the steps. You *are* moving forward. Recognize this. Remind yourself and give yourself praise for your achievement and in stepping forward in your life.

This is your turn-a-round. When you can give yourself praise and feel ok about it. When you can do this you know you'll make it. You'll be able to change those behavioural patterns which no longer serve you. You will become self confident with a healthy self esteem.

Look at what you're attracting to you through this process. Remember energy goes where attention flows. So what are you giving your attention to—right now, ask. Focus on how you want to be. See yourself as confident and radiant. Focus. Focus on this picture of you. Allow *you* to become radiant.

You need to begin to integrate your new focus, your affirmations, and your positive attitude into your daily life. See yourself this way <u>every morning.</u> Reaffirm throughout the day if you need to. Banish all self doubt. It will only pull you backwards. That's not where you want to be is it? So if self doubt creeps into your mind, be alert and push it away immediately. Don't give self doubt your energy.

Chapter Eight

The Secret Law of Financial Creation

This is something we all want, financial abundance. We think it will free us from all concerns in our lives. There are numerous books on this subject so why does financial abundance seem to only work for some people and not others? You buy books on abundance and read excitedly yet you still struggle with your bills. What is it that's missing? Master Kuthumi says,

> *"You're missing the point. It is your attitude that will determine how well you will receive."*

We are not meant to go without. Some are born with riches and abundance, others win it, some inherit it. They may have great lessons to learn about power. Because to have a lot of money is power. Some may come to a realization that they can 'buy' people as well as anything else they may want. Some become very selfish. Although they have a lot of money they don't really want to spend it. They like to show others their wealth stattice through their material possessions and often flaunt these, but they don't want to part with their money. They really see their money as power and have a fear of losing that power. Still others use their money to 'lord' it over others in a show of perceived greatness. They are able to do this in such a way as to make the person without a lot of money feel quite inadequate. All of these scenarios are total abuse of power.

Of course their ego self just loves it all. So you can see that there are certainly lessons around having a lot of money. The lessons can also come from your past life. If you were lazy and self indulgent in your last life then this time round you will experience the need to work hard for your money. Nothing will come easily to you until you learn a better attitude around money and the power it gives. Mmm, there's that word again—attitude. Well that covers some people, but what about the rest of us?

The Four Steps to Financial Abundance

There are four steps and here they are.

Step One:

Self Worth. This goes through to your own core belief around how you see yourself. Do you really see yourself as worthy of having lots of money? Lots of abundance? Or do you secretly think, "It'll never happen to me." Or, "I'll just have to keep working for my money." Remember the section on Do the Words? What are you telling the Universe? What are you reaffirming in your computer—the subconscious mind? You make sentences like these because you have a low self worth. You secretly feel unworthy of winning anything, or of being financially rich. You can make your Wish Board but you're going to sabotage yourself by thinking these thoughts. These thoughts and thoughts like them will prevent abundance from manifesting for you. So you'll stay in your yo-yo pattern of "Yes, I want money. And then—no it won't be me, I won't win. I won't succeed. I never do." Well, now you know why you don't. You're too busy self sabotaging yourself through your thoughts and words.

Step Two:

Bless Your Bills. This may sound strange but it's actually very powerful. I'll explain why. What do you normally do when a bill comes in? If it's a small one probably not much. But what about when a big bill arrives in your letter box? Usually the emotion is annoyance or fear. You may think," How can I pay this? Where's the money coming from? I don't have enough money. I can't afford this." Just stop for a moment and think how many times you are saying these words. Often women say when shopping, "I can't afford that. I don't have enough money."

> ## The Universe answers your words.

Yes, when you keep repeating words, the Universe will obey your request. I don't have enough money. I can't afford that. So what do you get? Not enough money. But isn't this what you're telling the Universe all the time? The Universe must answer. It's Universal Law. So now you see why I told you to always bless your bills. It's very powerful. Here's an affirmation to help you.

> ## I bless my bills. I now pay this bill quickly and efficiently with ease now.

Always add the 'now' when asking anything of the Universe. They don't work with our linear time you see. There is another affirmation I use a lot and I find it so helpful.

> ## Money comes quickly and easily to me now.

This always works well for me. I don't allow myself to worry about the bills. Trust the Universe and follow through with your emotions. Always bless your bills when they arrive.

Step Three:

Attitude. Master Kuthumi said this was your key. This *is* the secret to abundant creation—attitude. So what is *your* attitude to money? How do you feel about it? My mother frequently told me, "Money is the root of all evil." While that may or may not be true, it did begin to become one of my core truths. So no matter what this core truth was lying at the bottom of every issue to do with money that I had. The root of all evil. So it can't be good to have money. Therefore do I really want it?

I had to counteract that core truth and turn it around. I started with an affirmation.

Money is an energy exchange.

You see how these words totally perceive money in a different way? From, "It's evil," to "This can be used to help me in many wonderful ways." As your core truth changes, so does your attitude. One other thing I want to mention here. Notice the word power is not mentioned. That's not the purpose of money really. It's not how we should look at money either. Money is a form of energy exchange to be used in a positive way to assist us in life.

Step Four:

Visualize. Visualize, and then visualize some more. See yourself having all the money you need. Not necessarily want, but need. All your bills are paid. The money is sitting waiting to be used to pay those bills and to buy your dream home or nice car. You live debt free and comfortable, and are able to focus on other things. See it. Visualize it. Feel it. Always. Don't stop. It should be your core belief. Now you have money, use it wisely.

Give thanks to the Universe <u>each day</u> for your abundance in life.

All of these four steps come into play to attain abundance. It all comes down to attitude and gratitude. Your attitude to money, your attitude toward yourself, and . . . your attitude toward God. Let me ask, do believe it is your birthright to have financial abundance? Do you blame God/Universe/Source for not having what you want? Are you grateful for what you have now, even if it's less than you wish for?

Many Forms of Abundance are Available

It's important to ask yourself these questions or you could be planting huge weeds! Your attitude will determine if you will have the financial level you desire. Though money is a form of energy, the Universe also continually sends you abundance in many other ways. For example, a good deal for that new TV, something you really wanted appears to fall into your lap usually through someone else's generosity or a friend cleans out her closets and gives you some really nice new clothes. You enjoy a summer day. You have food and shelter. There are many, many ways the Universe will use to bring you abundance.

You need to practice *gratitude* also. I have a Chinese string of coins hanging on the inside of my front door. Often as I go out, I grasp them and give thanks to the Universe for my abundance. I may have received no money that day but I know and truly believe that I receive abundance in many forms every day.

Abundance does come in many forms. The heat of the Sun, the green lush trees, a birds song, a beautiful flower in bloom, a reliable car to go to work in, feeling well. It's all abundance. That's how I see it. I constantly tell myself, "I have no lack." I do the words. I've learnt to. You can too.

You need to be consistent. Keep saying the words, keep visualizing what you want. No use just doing it for a week or two. Nothing may happen in that time. Don't go into the cave. Keep going forward. Don't become conditional to the Universe by saying through your actions, "I'll believe in you if you send me this, or that." That's totally conditional behaviour.

You wouldn't like your friends and work mates putting conditions on their friendship would you? You know the sort. I'll accept you only if you comply with what I want you to do, or to be. Hard as it may be, those who seek conditional relationships from you on any level aren't worthy of your energy—any of it. They are using the art of manipulation. Master Kuthumi says,

> *"By accepting their terms of relationship, you are aiding them to think that way about you and to treat you in a manipulative manner. So why do you think you can complain? You have allowed it to be. In many ways encouraged it by staying silent and accepting that type of behaviour."*

Interesting words. But back to financial creation and it's just that—creation. Because whatever idea or image you hold in your mind repeatedly it will come to you. Like attracts like. It's a very powerful force isn't it?

**Problems are just opportunities
for learning in disguise.**

Information filters through to your conscious mind through the five senses—smell, taste, feeling, seeing and hearing. Sometimes though our senses will deceive us. So we gather false information which in turn can become false beliefs. For instance, you may think you heard a certain thing but actually you didn't. Or you may think you saw something. But you only saw a small window of happenings and not the full picture, so false information. But you have gathered this information from your outer world which is outside of you.

Your Core Truths

Your truth is held within you. Always has been. Yet many fail to see this. You always need to connect to your heart and your higher self which merges with your heart. Listen to your feelings. They are your higher guidance. Your conscious mind filters data through to your sub-conscious mind. What I call the computer. It's really only as good as the data which is consistently and consciously fed into it. So let's think about what it is you are constantly feeding your mind. What core truths are you forming?

Think about this. This is the **core process**. This is how everything works. Think of yourself as the computer programmer. Think about what you have programmed around the issue of money and the issue of receiving abundance. Is your sub-conscious working for or against you? Are you sabotaging your own abundance?

The sum total of this determines your personal level of financial abundance and awareness. If you look at this now and the effects, you will be able to evaluate if this is happening to you. Sometimes you go on quite blindly until you take a look, evaluate and tweak if necessary to make positive adjustments. You may even have to change some behavioural patterns that no longer serve you. Ones you've outgrown. See this as a growing process and celebrate.

Your sub-conscious mind is the trigger that will bring to you what it sees as your desire. So you can see how important it is to pause and to look at what you have programmed in to your sub-conscious computer. What has become your core truth? Your sub-conscious mind will also draw to you situations and people in order to *bring you your desire*. This is huge. Let's think about this for a moment.

Look at the scenario that you don't really like Chris. Every time you think of Chris—which seems to be often—you have very coloured and negative thoughts about him. You might see his manipulation, greed, smart comments above everything else. They begin to act out and play in your conscious mind. Funny thing is Chris seems to keep coming into your life and always pushes your buttons making you angry and upset very quickly. When he leaves you again play out little things in you mind about him, this time with more negative energy.

The pattern keeps repeating with one difference. Your anger toward Chris keeps building. That's because you keep feeding those negative thought patterns and attitude toward Chris. All this then feeds into your sub-conscious mind because you think negatively about Chris so much. This then develops into a core truth, so you will always see Chris in a negative way. Because you are thinking of Chris so much your dutiful sub-conscious constantly brings Chris into your life, and the circle continues.

Do you see? This is how our minds work. If you have low self esteem rooted in your sub-conscious, you be continually presented with issues reinforcing your core belief of a low self esteem. Your sub-conscious, working with the Universe, will bring you repeated failures. So it becomes an endless cycle until you realize. *You* are creating this cycle of failure. STOP!

Look closely at Your Self Talk

Time to look at your self talk now, your thoughts and your focus. It's really good to use affirmations. These are wonderful. They are positive energy feeding into your sub-conscious mind. Remember the song 'Don't worry, be happy.' Even saying it brings a form of calmness. You can say this whenever you get into a worry mode. Just keep repeating it over and over. You'll soon lighten up. That's because you're telling your mind to be happy and not to worry. You can even write it on a piece of paper as a visual reminder.

I remember when I first started telling people you create your reality. Some only partly understood. But anyone can do this. The Universe supports your higher reality, the reality related through your heart centre. This doesn't hurt or use anyone else. There are two kinds I feel. There's the reality created through your conscious words and actions. This is the flow on effect. Like ripples through a pond of water. The effects flow out to others.

Then there's the reality the Universe takes a big hand in to create with you. This comes under the basic Laws of Creation. This happens when you are naturally in the *state of gratitude*. Gratitude flows from an open heart. A heart which sees beyond physical existence. A heart which is enriched from the flow of the higher self fuelled by the soul. Yes it is possible to create, oh yes. But many still think they can just snap their fingers and wham! It's there. Creation is much deeper than that expectation.

To succeed you also need to focus and have a certain amount of self discipline. No good deciding on something then changing your mind. Think of your sub-conscious as a servant. It simply carries out your bidding and your focused desire.

By now you may have begun to make some changes in your life while reading this book. You now know you *can* do it. You have the tools to succeed. Use your new knowledge of the cave ladder, the affirmations, the Can Do button and visualization, all the tools here. The only thing that will stop you is you. True! You have great power within you to succeed. You equally have great power to self sabotage.

There may be times when you will step back into old modes of belief and behaviour. Don't stop there. Don't completely sabotage yourself. Learn from your mistake or whatever it was that created the need to go into old mode behaviour. Look at it honestly. Look at the _cause._ What was it? That's what you need to address. Not the outcome. The _cause._

Steps to Release All Fear

The Universe is giving you an opportunity to learn, to grow and to step forward. Grab it! Problems are really opportunities in disguise. Grab that abundance ladder in one hand and your Can Do man in the other hand. Take a deep breathe, draw back your shoulders say I CAN DO IT! Then do it, step by step. Don't see the mountain, only see each step.

New scientific evidence has proven that your mental process, mental state, and mental behaviours affect all the cells in your body constantly. Electrical impulses in the body carry information through your nerve cells. These are called Neurons. There are also small gaps between any two Neurons called a Synapse. As the impulses travel along some help to cross a Synapse. Neuro transmitters complete this task in carrying electrical impulses across the Synapses between nerve cells. These Neuro transmitters cover every cell in our body. Scientists now acknowledge the mind body connection.

Understand the sub conscious mind manages body functions, sensations, movements and sends information to the billions of cells throughout your body. Your immune system is constantly affected by the unconscious mind. Everyone has this. When you understand the process, there is no need to fear anything.

Fear is created in your outer world by others, usually for control of a situation, an event, or you! Why buy into it? Instead I suggest you work on your inner world through your sub conscious mind.

The Law of Cause and Effect

You could say your sub conscious mind provides the cause through your core truths, and your conscious mind plays out the effect—the repercussion of the cause. Let's take this a step further. We are often unaware of our sub conscious mind and all the core truths it holds until a scenario is played out around us which upsets us to various degrees. The variance of upset tells us how deeply an emotional 'button' has been pushed. You get angry, upset and frustrated. When this happens you need to pause. *Don't focus on the problem, focus on the cause.*

What is your core truth around the issue? What exactly is the issue? Is it feeling a loss of control, is it being over looked or feeling not good enough? Is it an issue of anger? What is the core issue that triggered your response? You will only find the answer when you go within. The answer isn't outside of you.

Some people have said this is karma. Well, there is another part to karma. That is the programming of your sub conscious mind. Cause and effect. It has been said many times the Light will set your free and it will. However understanding your sub conscious mind will help you fly. When you understand this process you are free to live a life of happiness and fulfilment.

Allow Yourself to Receive

I want to talk now about receiving. It's important to allow yourself to receive. Many are unable to do this. These people usually give so much to others yet feel unable to accept the smallest gift themselves. By not accepting however they take away the pleasure the other person feels in giving.

Allow all things to be in balance, to give and to receive. Of course by giving all the time, particularly to one person, you create a karmic debt to that person. Where is the energy exchange and the balance? One person is doing all the giving. You are worthy of receiving. The core truth here in this situation above, is feeling unworthy of receiving. So you need to change that core belief if this applies to you. You are the computer programmer. You are in charge. You create your own reality. Here are some affirmations to help with this situation. Spread your arms open wide when you say this one. You'll feel why. It's really good to say one of these every morning.

> **I am a perfect child of the universe and I open myself now to receive.**

> **I am worthy of total abundance in my life and I receive willingly with love.**

Repeat either of these, or both, as often as you can opening your arms wide as you do so. Reprogram the computer. Go within and ask why you have this core truth about receiving. Who gave you this core truth? Someone did. You decided to accept it and to take it on board as your own truth. But it's done. Now it's time to focus on *you*. To focus on *your success*. Here is a release exercise given to me by Master Kuthumi. Are you ready? Here we go.

The Release and Focus Meditation

As before take the phone off the hook and shut the door. Try not to be disturbed. If you have a special meditation space sit in that space now. Be comfortable.

Complete Kuthumi's 3 breath exercise as before. This aligns your subtle bodies.

Relax your physical body. Begin with the leg muscles and release them.

Move on to your tummy muscles and your chest and release them.

Now those large shoulder muscles, release them. As you do so, feel your arms and hands relaxing and begin to feel quite heavy in your lap.

Release your facial muscles. Feel any remaining thoughts moving away from you, getting quieter and quieter. Relax. Breathe . . . . in . . . . and out . . . .

Focus on who told you these words which you have claimed as a core truth. Do you remember who?

Now tell them that this is their truth and it's no longer your truth. It doesn't fit in your life any longer. You've moved on. It doesn't belong to you any more.

Try to visualize two large hands before you, taking back the core truth. Let it go. It's not yours and never really was.

Now see yourself surrounded in golden Light. You are so bright. You are glowing.

Breathe in that beautiful Light.

Bring that golden Light into your heart centre, feel it.

Now say to yourself in your mind, I am worthy of total abundance in my life now. I receive now with love. You may repeat this if you wish.

Rest in the Light.

Now give thanks to the Universe for all that you have and all that will come to you.

See yourself in a beautiful large ball of white Light.

Now gently open your eyes and come back to awareness.

The keys are focus and trust. These are essential. You also need to say the two previous affirmations often to create your new core belief. If you truly believe you are worthy, you will notice many levels of abundance entering your life, not just monetary.

Assumption Avenue

You all know our planet is in the process of a great shift in energy. Some call it a shift in consciousness which it is, but consciousness is energy. Many carry and hold onto fear creating great insecurity around them. Yet much of that fear is based on tomorrow. That feeling of insecurity leads on to Assumption Avenue. What if this, what if that. Maybe this, maybe that. These scenarios are not around you, they haven't happened. Yet so much energy is wasted on assuming. These assumptions are based on fear.

Have you noticed that every thought in Assumption Avenue is a negative one? Why do you suppose that is? There are two reasons. One is fear as I mentioned and the other is ego. They play a game of chase. They chase each other in an endless circle going round and round, getting bigger and bigger because they're being fed with all the energy you're giving them. Assumption Avenue is similar to the cave. It's a different place though because in Assumption Avenue you play out an imagined future. Sadly it's usually a negative future which is played out in your conscious mind.

You're busy trying to work everything out absorbing and recalling all those negative comments you heard or read from everyone else outside of you. Then you embellish those mind pictures with more future scenarios. Because you give energy to fear, you allow it to manifest within your mind.

Do you remember way back at the beginning of this book when you threw out the unstable blocks in your foundation and we went on to weed your inner garden? You felt strong then didn't you? Do you remember when I said you need a really strong foundation so that when a storm hits your strength and confidence wouldn't tumble down or be washed away?

Well, we're in a bit of a storm here on Earth now. We're right in the middle of a huge transition in consciousness. We are being asked to review our inner beliefs. We are being asked to listen to our soul and to remember. We are being asked to think less and feel more. We are being asked to awaken our power centres and our sacred minds. Every one of us has to do the inner work to get to that point. But . . . it's so worth it.

Sometimes you may think it's a lot easier to just ignore the inner work. Just to hope it will go away and everything will be ok. You know it won't be don't you? Sometimes the Universe steps in using the planetary energies or even other people to give you a bit of a 'shake and wake' experience. When this occurs, there's usually something happening in your life that makes you feel uncomfortable, even threatened. Know it will get worse until you stop, think and wake up to face something that needs changing, and it's usually your conscious attitude and thinking. Even sometimes misplaced priorities.

This is happening right now through the world monetary system, relationship issues and too much focus on material items. You're not alone with all these questions and inner clearing. This book gives you many tools to help you through this great cycle of change on Earth.

So you see there is great polarity in creation—your creation. What you think becomes real, it becomes an action. What you focus on often comes to you. You draw it to you via your sub-conscious mind. 85% of what you do stems from the sub-conscious mind, the computer. So at this point ask yourself what type of computer technician are you? What is programmed into your computer which no longer serves you?

The Sacred Mind

Here is a way to stretch your mind to be able to look at any problem and to perceive Creator Conscious outcomes. Yes, you **Can Do** it! I'll show you how. Stay with me.

Have you caught yourself day dreaming, or having just driven past your turn off on the motorway without realizing and then becoming alert and wondering how you did that? That is expanding your mind. You can function physically but your mind may be elsewhere on another level. The brain is quite capable of working on many levels at once. Some may have difficulty at first in reaching this expansive state of mind. You can achieve it when you meditate also. You rise above the conscious mind beyond Theta and Delta waves. You must be completely relaxed so it's important your physical body is comfortable when meditating.

When you bring a problem to this expansive state your brain is searching the soul memory for new information, often extending to the super conscious brain for higher answers allowing you to find and see soul solutions. Often solutions coming from this part of your brain connect to the higher source of consciousness. Total relaxation is the key to attain this.

With practice you can reach this higher state of awareness easily. You can then attain your higher conscious mind readily at any time you wish. The answers you receive will be beyond any ego. Therefore you will be shown a higher perspective to your problem whatever that may be. You will feel an altered state of consciousness. Your physical body will feel relaxed and quite heavy. You will feel peaceful and often a little 'spacey' at first as your body adjusts to a higher frequency of vibration. You may well perceive what you thought was a giant unsolvable problem for you, is now a very small and insignificant one.

This is because you have been using your higher conscious mind, connecting to Source consciousness. You may also feel slightly sleepy. I often feel sleepy after trance channelling with Master Kuthumi. I feel a little like a rag doll too as I'm just so relaxed.

This feeling can last some time as the energies filter through to your physical body and conscious awareness. It's an adjustment period while the higher energies filter through you. Remember you are a multi-dimensional being but all energy must come through to the physical body eventually. You are not limited to your conscious mind or your physical body. You are much more than these.

If you take all those emotions and states of being you experienced from Assumption Avenue you would see what a negative, futile state of being it really is. You would see it is based on conscious thoughts through ego and fear. Negative emotions grown so large they consume you and threaten to take over your life.

I wrote a poem on the front page of our web site called, 'I am a Creator." www.kuthumischool.com

It was inspired by a song I heard. But I *am* a creator. You are too. Practice going into your higher consciousness. Take *all* your problems there and *listen* to your inner feelings as your soul speaks to you. Be still. You will then easily overcome problems in your daily life with help from above. After all, we are entering a time on Earth of as above, so below.

Chapter Nine

As Above, So Below

We have discussed the Higher Mind which the Pineal Gland works through and which also contains the Crown Vortex. Remember that all those energies and visions that you experience in your Soul Light—when you are in a higher state of awareness—must be filtered down through the subtle bodies to the physical body. Now you can see why your thoughts are so important. There's a whole world out there beyond this physical world. But you don't see it with your physical eyes. You have to use your 6th sense, your feeling heart and your soul knowledge.

Your Deliberate Creation

A while back we spoke of releasing all lack on all levels. We spoke of how your childhood conditioning can affect if and how you will receive financial abundance in your life. Your past life experience comes into the picture as well. You may be thinking, "Well, I haven't got a chance." But you do! When we began I told you everything was energy, including you. When you go through an energetic shift it is subtle and normally raises your current energy level so your vibrational level becomes higher and finer. The energy shift itself is subtle, yet you *can* feel it. You may have experienced emotional turmoil preceding the shift because usually it is necessary to let go of lower vibrations in order for the actual shift in energy to occur. The release may be in your thinking, a behaviour pattern or someone close to you who is 'reflecting' on to you. Remember the ripple effect? You can be caught in that ripple. In other words, if someone close is continually negative that negative energy can ripple on to you. Therefore the negativity must be released from your emotional body before the shift can occur.

Some people do new moon meditations. The new moon is the moon of creation. If you are beginning a new venture the first three days after the new moon are very potent for manifesting those new wishes and plans into being. And that's it! Manifesting energy! You manifest what you desire using the powerful new moon rays. You visualize it as clearly as you can in every detail. You see yourself having it, what you would do, how you would look. You see yourself happy. Visualize, make it important on your manifestation list. If your wish is for financial gain imagine what you would do with your money. How much would you need? Be specific. If you're paying for a house see yourself closing the deal with the mortgage papers in your hand. What does your house look like? How many rooms? Are they large rooms or small rooms? What colour is the house? Does it have a garden? Is the land fenced? See it. Create it! You are creating your life on a new level in the higher realms. There are two more steps which we have discussed, but they are an extremely important part of this process.

1. <u>Know</u> you are worthy of this—no doubts. You have to know and believe you <u>do</u> deserve this—every bit of it.
2. <u>Focus</u>. Begin the Focus Meditation on a new moon, but don't stop there. Each time you meditate visualize it again and see yourself having your desire. Perhaps not as much time as you spent on the new moon meditation, but finish seeing your desire and having it. Knowing is so important. Knowing it will come to you.

Try this affirmation:

> **I have no lack financial**
> **abundance comes to me now**
> **I am debt free now.**

Affirmations work on the sub conscious. We know the Masters manifest at will. But remember they operate at a much higher level of vibration. In a meditative state you rise above the mundane of daily life. You rise above all the problems of the outer world to gain the meaning and answers to your life from a higher perspective.

Here is a new moon meditation for you.

New Moon Focus Meditation

It is good to have an idea of what you want to create or what project you wish to begin before you meditate.

As before take the phone off the hook and shut the door. Try not to be disturbed. If you have a special meditation space sit in that space now. Be comfortable.

Complete Kuthumi's 3 breath exercise as before.

Relax your physical body. Begin with the leg muscles, let them go and feel them relax.

Move on to relax your tummy muscles and your chest. Now those large shoulder muscles, let them go. As you do so, feel your arms and hands relaxing and feel quite heavy in your lap.

Let go of your facial muscles. Feel any remaining thoughts moving away from you, getting quieter and quieter. Relax. Breathe . . . . in . . . . and out . . . .

One wish of creation at a time . . . .
Ask—see it
How does it look? Give the Universe details—as many as you can

See yourself achieving or having it and truly believe it will be so
Ask the Universe to bring it to you now.
Go onto your next wish and repeat the process

When you've finished always give thanks

Now visualize bringing a beautiful clear pyramid over you. See yourself inside the pyramid, safe and loved.

Open your eyes.
You are now present once more.

The Still Voice Within Awaits

When you reach this point it is wise to be aware and to listen to your own 'inner voice.' Sometimes your 'inner voice' will speak to you through your feelings. You will get a feeling to phone a certain person for example. Or you may suddenly feel whether a person is trust worthy or not. This feeling is noticeable and you just seem to feel and know all at once. At other times you may take a dislike to a person you've only just met. They may have said or done nothing to you at that time. Always listen to these feelings. This is your own intuition at work. In this latter instance you had a negative experience with that person, usually in a previous life time, but the soul remembers and seeks to warn you.

When you begin to do this you will find yourself becoming more aware of your sixth sense, your intuition. You will need to be relaxed. For some this will come easily, for others it will take more practice. Every one is different. There are no rules. Much not only depends on your attitude and experiences in this lifetime, but also on your past lifetime as well. For instance, you may have been psychic in your previous life time so you have decided—before incarnating—that you will simply just open to spirit and continue your higher path.

Some people are transcentient. That is they smell spirit. You could smell cigar smoke for example, though no one is smoking a cigar in the room. You could smell lavender perfume or home baking. Any of these smells could be related to someone you knew who has passed over (died.) During their life they may have loved baking, worn a certain perfume or smoked cigars. All of these are very different yet in each case it is your own psychic ability communicating to you. So you do need to be aware. Remember not every one will work psychically the same way.

What Really Is the Secret?

There has been much speculation since The Secret video was released. What is it really? What are we to believe? Do the answers to life lie inside of us or outside? Of course the answers lie within each of us. All we need is within us. Master Kuthumi says there is one word that is the secret for all of us. That word is **Believe!**

Believe you are worthy and believe in yourself. Believe and it will be so. Believe. This one word may test your faith and the strength of your foundation blocks. However you need to ask yourself how the Masters are able to manifest at will—instantly. Why is that? It is because of two things. Because they believe. They know with absolutely no doubt that it will be so. They *will* receive it. This belief coupled with their higher energy manifests all they desire in their realm.

We have this ability also. We do. But we still have ingrained within us the belief that we don't have this power. As long as you hold a small fragment of this belief you won't!

Teleportation of Matter

It's just energy—shifting from one place to another or making yourself invisible. First you must believe and totally fill yourself with pure unconditional love. A love so strong you are lifted to a very high energy frequency. Remember everything is energy. To shift the heavy matter of your body you need to vibrate at a high frequency of energy. The emotion of unconditional love greatly assists with this frequency. Without this, you will not be of the correct vibrational level to shift matter.

There are already Light workers on the planet who are practicing the art of teleportation. They are fully aware of spirit, of matter and of the various levels of energy. It's part of Quantum Psychics. One day we'll all be able to do this but right now we are still in the kindergarten stage of this development and understanding. We need to do a lot more forgiving, a lot more loving and become a lot more compassionate to all living things. When we don't just become aware of this, when we actually live this way without thinking about it, then we may radiate at the vibrational frequency required. It will require great change for many and also great practice. Many don't believe they are capable of moving themselves from one place to another—teleportation. But we are quite capable. We *do* have **_unlimited potential._**

Confusion around 'The Shift'

Some people feel they are still confused about the shift we underwent on 21 December 2012. Many don't understand the conscious shift mankind has already entered into. Others don't want to know and are in denial. Some are in an altered ego state and believe they are the new 'guru's.' Still others just aren't sure what to think. So this creates a state of confusion in the world. However there is hope as confusion usually precedes a state of higher learning. As Master Kuthumi says," *Understanding releases fear.*" It's true. When we understand a process—of anything—that knowledge and understanding releases any fear we may have been holding on to. That's why it's been so important for you to work through this book, gaining a deeper understanding of the process of transformation.

Until you work through, from your foundation level upwards, to a level of deeper understanding, of acknowledging feelings, of experiencing, you cannot transcend to the Light. Your bodies, all seven of them, need to be prepared to carry a great deal of Light particles. So much so that all of us will eventually glow due to the pure Light energy we will carry within us. This is what we are heading toward. That's why this cycle in mankind's evolution is different.

But is it Enough?

Is it enough to know why and to have an understanding of higher awareness and Light energy? If we are prepared to take action then yes, it is.

But let me ask you now, when was the last time you took action to change a behavioural pattern, or to release a long held negative memory? Many find it so much easier to simply go back to the same old behaviour. So you fail to get a different result.

> **Nothing changes, if
> nothing changes.**

You may know how, when, why, but you continue to replicate old behaviour. Why is this? Usually again because of fear, yes fear.

People fear a confrontation that would necessitate change; they think it would be too uncomfortable. People fear communication—both external and in their conscious mind. It's all too difficult. Yet if you know within you it's time to take action then regardless of how you feel start changing your perception and just do it! Perception is creation. Don't allow what's hurt you in the past to limit your growth now. You are no longer that same person. You have the tools and the knowledge to move forward into a powerful future— don't say I can't, say *I can!*

The Polarity of Thought

We all really need to look within our own thought process from time to time. We all have a choice of negative or positive thoughts. We have *total and absolute control* over our own thought process 24/7.

To change the polarity of thought requires self discipline just as it requires self discipline to change unwanted behaviour patterns. It's up to you. No one can do it for you.

What is your truth may not be another's. Or they may see the same truth in a different way, or they may believe in only half of your truth. To say things must be done they way **you** want is coming from the ego self. Yet in this there is a great learning opportunity. Because this allows you to see the process of transformation step by step. It is transformation of thought, of belief, of core truths, and feeling compassion for your fellow man by accepting they have a right to their opinion and way of doing things.

Your mind controls your emotional body. What you think, how you think, your thinking process affects how you feel which in turn controls how you will react. So you see you have the power to control each response each day, month, year, lifetime.

As you grow spiritually and as a person, your response will change. It changes because of the experiences you choose to draw to yourself. You're thinking process changes and your emotional process changes.

What Do You Bring To You?

This is interesting. Many have difficulty in accepting that you choose every experience. You actually draw it to you through thought and intention. Sometimes it is a karmic or pre birth contractual experience. But many of those smaller every day experiences you actually choose. You also choose how you will respond to them. This is important because it depicts the spectrum of Light within you and therefore your state of higher consciousness.

Will you respond with anger, annoyance, neutrality, tears, frustration, or love? Will you respond at all? How much energy will you use in your response and what sort of energy will it be? Positive or negative? You choose. You decide. *And in that decision you decide if you will draw that experience to you.*

If it is you personally creating this experience, then you have already chosen so you obviously need all the learning aspects the experience will bring to you at that time. If it is coming from someone else in your outer world then you do indeed have a choice through your response.

It all comes down to your response and your choice. I find this quite amazing. It is so true but we don't really think about our daily life in these terms very much do we? We have been programmed to simply accept that it's life so just put up with it. In our mental separateness we are told to survive as best we can. *We are told.* Where is *our own* mental, emotional and spiritual process in all of this? Have we become robots?

Much of what is presented to us by other people we don't have to accept or experience. We may choose whether what we hear is right or not—to us. We choose how much energy to give to a situation presented to us. *We choose.* If we give it lots of energy then we draw that experience closer to us. We buy into it. For better or for worse, we've decide to be in there.

> **Whatever you draw to you depends on how much energy you choose to give it.**

So many along the way are hard on themselves and they really emotionally beat themselves up. And they also love to regurgitate it all over again and again, so they beat themselves up some more as they go over every detail. They give the experience so much energy. But it has become stagnant energy. They try to keep the experience alive by giving it more and more emotional energy over time.

What is important is what you have learnt from the experience. What do you take from the experience and how do you choose to deal with the experience emotionally? This is your purpose for incarnating on Earth. To experience duality and in that experience choose your reaction. Balance is the key to success. You learn to balance your mind, your emotions and your actions through choice.

Through this learning and the experiences of life you learn detachment from all the many and varied distractions of the material world. As you learn this you raise your vibration immensely and connect once more to Divine Consciousness.

Do you Take Responsibility?

Through all of this you begin to take responsibility for yourself and your actions. You choose your own path. In that responsibility and awareness you begin to embody that awareness into your speech and actions. You are aware of behaving in a responsible manner to all other living beings on Earth. You develop a better attitude to life and to others. You begin to notice the beauty in others instead of faults and short comings. You gain a higher perception of everything around you.

You understand and appreciate yourself in a new light. You begin to actually love yourself again. Most people have difficulty with this concept. They've forgotten what their soul has always known. But as you take responsibility for yourself, your words and actions, your attitude of <u>you</u> changes as well. Because you are more aware you raise your vibration. This also frees your Mental Body to begin operating from your Higher Mental Body. The Higher Mental Body opens the door to God Consciousness. This process frees you from the lower Mental Body and thought process. And so you continue to gain more and more higher awareness and to hold more Light energy within. Gratitude and compassion flow freely around and through you.

Chapter Ten

Enjoy Fabulous Relationships

How do you Communicate?

Now we will take a look at various types of relationships. Let's begin with you! In the first chapter I asked you to write a list of four things you wanted to change about yourself. Remember? Have you loved yourself enough to make the changes you desire?

In the past you may have made excuses to yourself. Excuses like "I'll do it later." There are so many times we simply sell ourselves short. You also looked at the people that had made a difference in your life and had helped you in a significant way through a difficult time or just made you feel special just when you needed it. You were asked to think of those friends you enjoyed spending your time with. Friends can be anyone even family members. In fact that's when they're really special friends. It's probably those special friends who have taught you valuable lessons of life and also how to *be* a friend.

A friend is someone very special. Many will tell you to have a good friend is like finding a pearl—rare and quite beautiful. There are so many people who just get caught up in their own lives. They are always too busy to visit, to share or to listen. Eventually you get the message that they don't think of you as very important at all.

Yet they may not feel this way about you. Often they just expect you to be there, waiting with a willing ear and compassion in your heart, to take the time to be there for them when they need you. To listen, to sympathize or to congratulate them on an achievement. I call this group the 'ME' friends. They really just care about themselves first and foremost. Everyone else has to fit into their needs. Problem is people soon tire of the one way street relationship and begin looking elsewhere for someone who will truly share.

Then there's the USERS group. You know the ones. Can you do this, will you pick up that, lend me a few dollars til payday, pick me up at 5pm. They simply expect you to do it. It's very convenient for *them*. Unfortunately not so convenient for you but you may not be ready to see that yet.

These ones are very clever. They usually sense when you're beginning to get annoyed and that's when they do something really nice for you or they are noticeably very kind to you. And what do you do? You melt of course and find those words," Oh, it's ok" begin flowing out of your mouth. They are charmers and they know how to play the game.

It does tend to go round in circles. The main problem here is that you feel you just *have* to keep doing all the things you're asked to do just to keep the friendship. If you don't do these things there is a deep seated fear within that they won't like you anymore. So you keep bowing to their whims, but after a time resentment begins to build within you. Those few showers of kindness from your friend don't quite do it anymore. You begin to notice more and more that one way street of your friendship. The resentments keep building.

At this point you have to ask yourself how important is this friendship to you? How important is this person to you? You are now faced with a decision. Do you talk to your friend? Will they actually listen or will they just pretend to listen but nothing will change?

Most people will begin to walk away and distance themselves. Eventually the two of you will grow apart. This happens in love partnerships as well. It just becomes too hard to say, "Time out. Let's talk about us." You need to be honest. Honest with yourself and honest with your partner. If you're not then you cheat yourself and the relationship.

Let's look at Catherine. Catherine knew there was a problem but she couldn't face it. So she buried her head in the sand like the Ostrich and hoped it would all go away. It didn't so she started being secretive and became too busy to visit. She was moving away from the relationship because she felt unable to speak her truth. How sad. She made the decision to give up on the relationship rather then sit down and work it out. That to Catherine was just too difficult. So she let it go. But worse was to come! Catherine began talking negatively about her now 'past' friend. She found fault and told everyone. These were not new faults. They had always been there. Catherine was aware of them and had put up with them for some time.

What Catherine was doing now was justifying herself. By finding faults in her old friend she was saying to others that it wasn't her fault the friendship had ended, it was her friend's behaviour. In Catherine's conscious mind she remained blameless and her criticism justified her decision to end the relationship and also justified her attitude and her consequent actions.

If you stop and look you can see this scenario played out time and time again. Each one played a part at the very beginning. Neither one set boundaries. They didn't begin the relationship on middle ground. One took repeatedly and expected the other to give repeatedly.

Love Relationships

Sometimes this early stage of a relationship is called the 'honeymoon' stage. This is because you are so happy, you have a new love, and you want to do all you can for them. So you tend to overlook any problems or behaviour faults. You make excuses for them. After all, you don't want to lose this person so better to just be quiet and to ignore those signs however small that you are noticing. In any relationship there is a leader and a follower. Rarely will a relationship with two leaders survive. Each will seek to dominate the other. Eventually if it is to last, one must submit even if only a little. This can also produce a love/hate relationship, where compromise is a dirty word.

In any relationship boundaries need to be set from the beginning. We all know we should do this yet so many can't or won't. So how can we have a fabulous relationship?

Let's look at the first step. This applies to any level of relationship whether friend, love, parent or child. You need to look at what the other person wants out of the relationship. What is it they really want? What do they expect of you, and from you? This is where you need to look to begin the process of setting boundaries. Boundaries are really guidelines. You need to love yourself enough and to care about yourself enough to do it.

Sometimes you can give the other person what they want without any bother. It may be that just having you around makes them feel secure. Or they may need the affection you are able to give them. It may be your sense of humour they like. There are a number of attributes which can apply here. There are many varied positive and negative needs of another who has entered your path of life. What you need to ask yourself is this. How much of what they want are you prepared to give them?

It's an important question which needs to be answered if any form of a relationship is to survive a long time. If you can't answer the question about a relationship around you then you will eventually pay a price. However if both parties are giving to each other mentally and emotionally then you do indeed have a pearl. Yes it's true. Genuine friends are like jewels to be appreciated, respected, admired and enjoyed.

On the other hand, if someone can't or won't answer the question it's usually because they just don't want to look at themselves or to change. Yet they feel they just have to be of service to everyone. Their friends, their partners, workmates, everyone because that's what they do. If they can't do that then no one will like them. The underlying cause here is self esteem. How can you overcome this? If this is you, you may see it not as a step, but a mountain.

Ok, let's begin with the first step to take you forward. What is your internal dialogue telling you? Very often it's quite negative and really putting you down. You criticize your speech, how you said it, what you said. And your actions are also included. There is not a lot of positive dialogue in your mind about you at all.

This is low self esteem. You have programmed your sub conscious mind, the computer, to believe that you are not worthy of others affections. Nothing you say or do is right. This is really cave language at its worst! You are so busy telling yourself you'll never succeed and certainly never be worthy so you live in victim mode, feeling you really are just not good enough.

In this situation you usually shrink into your cave away from everyone. Then a friend comes along and up goes the service flag again. You think, "I must work hard to be accepted and to make them happy with me." So you reinforce to yourself again believing if you work really hard you will somehow overcome these destructive thoughts and feelings. To this end you will usually become a very hard task master of yourself. But what can you do?

Use the Soul Wash meditation again, and again. As many times as you need until you *feel* a change of attitude within you. It's on page eight. Work through the steps one at a time. Get out the CAN DO button you made. Keep him close as a reminder.

Acknowledge and reward *every* step you take successfully no matter how small. Small steps precede big steps. When you are in the cave you have no clarity of thought, only confusion. You may feel quite scattered, unable to concentrate and low in energy. Recognize it—80%. Remember the other 20% is working on a solution! Use this affirmation to help you from Master Kuthumi.

> **I deserve and claim the full
> abundance of the Universe now
> I am worthy of this**

Keep repeating this affirmation. Put it everywhere, on mirrors, on the fridge, work desk, car dash, everywhere you can. Say it, repeat it. Scientists have proven 85% of our thoughts are negative. Isn't that terrible? Turn it around. Be part of the other 15% with positive thoughts and good self esteem. Use the many tools and affirmations given to you in this book. Remember the 'delete' word? Use it every time you catch yourself in old behaviour and old terminology. Be like an athlete, committed to yourself. Practise, practise and practise. You're worth it aren't you? Become aware of what type of thoughts you're feeding your mind and your soul.

Take Responsibility for Your Thoughts

Yes, it's that word again. But you need to take responsibility for yourself, your thoughts and your actions. Focus on your achievements.

Write a list—a long list—of all the wonderful things you do in a day, or a week. These are significant achievements. Acknowledge them and begin building up your self esteem. Begin to see the opportunities you missed because you felt you weren't good enough. You will soon begin seeing yourself differently.

Listening Correctly is a Skill

There are many books and classes available for speaking but very few for listening correctly. So often people think they heard someone say something, only to find that's not what they actually said at all. They said something entirely different.

Listening is a skill. Many need to attune their sense of hearing and this takes awareness and practise. Just try for one morning <u>really</u> listening. Really focusing on someone's words as they speak to you. You will probably find you feel quite tired. That's because you're not used to really listening. Often we think we're listening but we often skim over the conversation we hear. Our conscious mind roles over events of the day and we use our eyes, sometimes thinking critically of how the person looks or how they're talking. All this happens at the same time. However in the translation you didn't hear all you think you heard. The eyes are very powerful receptors; the ears are not so strong. We are able to <u>believe</u> we heard what we wanted to hear. This also shows you how cunning the ego self can be.

We can overcome the ego self influencing what we hear. We can become aware and practise. Just like any other part of your body your hearing can be exercised as well. Focus on listening clearly to all your conversations for three weeks. The body, the wonderful machine that it is, will remember what you have trained it to do and you will find you are listening much more closely than before. You may be amazed at just how clearly you now listen, or how much your 'monkey mind' was playing in many conversations.

Methods of Conversation

We communicate in other ways besides speaking and listening. We use body language a great deal, often without even realizing our body is saying what we aren't. People who have studied body language will tell you this.

Do you realize that many problems in family and work relationships are because the other person does not clearly understand your message? Perhaps you may suddenly go into defensive mode and say, "Well that's their problem, I told them."

And there is the first step toward confrontation. We need to learn how to communicate to one another. How you communicate is the key to every form of relationship you have. Even when you are in a foreign country and don't speak the language very well you can smile. A smile is universal. It crosses all communication barriers. Why? It's friendly and non-threatening. It says," I like you." It puts people at ease. Conversely think for a moment of speaking to someone who is straight faced with no expression at all. Then they cross their arms. What is that telling you? Their body language is saying I don't agree with you, I'm closed to what you are saying.

Someone said to me once to say nothing is very powerful—and it is. At the right time if you stay silent people will turn to you and wait for you to speak. Imagine a seminar; the speaker gets up to speak. Everyone around is chattering. The speaker standing says nothing and waits. In a very short time the people notice and they fall silent. All eyes are now on the speaker who has gained their full attention without saying a word.

Another important example is simply listening to a friend who has a big problem in their life. They tell you all about it, every detail. How they feel and why they feel that way. What they think of the other person—all of it. This is a time when you really need to be still and just listen. By being there and doing this you are building a stronger relationship. You are showing support without judgement and without saying a word.

Listening properly is extremely important to good communication. It is also the most ignored. Please try during the next week to observe just how different people communicate with each other. It's interesting to watch and you can really learn a lot. Some will butt in without really listening but just itching to have their say. They just want to be centre stage in the conversation.

When a close partner thinks your not listening they can and do get very upset. Because by not listening and by clearly not wanting to listen you are saying what they have to say is not worthy enough for you to listen to. Mmm. Did you ever think of it this way? They feel this is a major put down. A huge insult because you are such an important person in their life.

The way you listen has a much bigger impact on your communication skills than talking. When you listen you show the person—I'm interested. You have all of my attention. Whether you agree or not will come out in the conversation, but you are listening to what they are saying. You are interested in them and how they think and feel. People sense this.

Indifference, not really listening, is extremely threatening to a person's self esteem. This type of behaviour creates huge gaps in a relationship. The one with low self esteem will usually withdraw even more, and go into either victim mode or servant mode thus feeding their low self esteem even more. They feel rejected and unworthy. Others will be more aggressive. In order to make you listen they may sleep on the couch, give you the 'silent treatment' and not talk at all for a period of time. Some wives often use this method on their husbands. And yes, it can be visa versa. A child often shouts angrily and throws a tantrum. Sometimes they pick a fight with a sibling. All to get your attention. They're saying silently, "You're not listening to me!"

In all of these examples the person is desperately trying to get your attention, even through negative behaviour. For children any attention is better than none. For adults they want you to pay attention and listen to them. To prove to them you think them special enough to listen to.

We can all be good listeners if we want to be. All people are important; they are interesting to observe and to listen to because we are all different with varying points of view. And it's not just in how people look, but how they feel, think and communicate. You can learn so much through simply listening clearly.

Your Commitment is Important

So we've looked at how important it is to communicate clearly, now let's look at commitment. This can mean commitment to various things like mowing the lawn, completing a successful sale, even being honest. But if I ask you how much are you committed to your relationship—either your love relationship or your best friend relationship, what would you say? Perhaps you'd go into defensive mode and too quickly tell me you're very committed. But are you?

You started out with intent of commitment, of staying with that person always, or being very best friends forever. Helping them through any difficulties they experience and always giving them your full support. However along the way with life's ups and downs your level of commitment got a bit battered. Perhaps you felt you didn't get enough support when you experienced difficulties in your life, or you found you were just too tired to give very much. After a hard day your partner or friend's problems were the last thing you needed to hear about. In any event, and probably a little of all the above, your level of commitment has wavered. You may have even found yourself saying in your last argument that you were sick and tired of hearing about their problems, or this place would fall to pieces if I left.

Resentment is setting in. Your computer, the unconscious mind, is recording every word. These words and emotions are adding to the previous judgments, criticisms, nasty comments that you've said or thought about this person previously. Now more is being recorded. The emotion of anger brews, getting stronger like an under ground volcano, building yet not shown on the surface. This anger may surface at a future conversation or comment with either your partner, friend or work colleague. Some will transfer their anger to others outside of the issue. Sometimes one small action from someone will lift that lid and the suppressed anger will spew forth.

Yes, this is all cave language. Do you remember the cave in the first chapter? This scenario happens to many over time. They say love is blind. Often people choose to 'flow' with the other person and to overlook those little habits and annoying behaviour patterns. We choose not to dwell on those traits we don't really like. We choose not to give them any of our energy. So what changes over time? Why is it that later in the relationship you find yourself shouting, arguing, sulking and blaming that person you felt so much love for that you chose to overlook his total personality early on?

First of all you know that you loved that person and you chose to commit to a relationship with that person. It doesn't matter if the person was a friend or partner. There was a level of trust. So when you had a really bad day or a life crisis you felt you could rely on that person to be there for you. But sometimes we go through hard testing. Tough experiences that last longer than a day or two. Usually the other person does as well. Maybe at some point the sharing and talking turned to silence and repressed anger. The communication has stopped from one of you. The cracks get larger as nasty verbal jibes are thrown at random.

But is the core of the issue really the person, or the job or financial security? So often you lash out at the person closest to you because you feel they'll put up with your anger. You go deep into the cave and cave language. Once begun it builds like a mini volcano. It's often a release and then you withdraw. What happens afterwards? There's usually a silence and quietness will settle in. Each will feel battered. The person doing all the shouting may feel quite remorseful but pride won't allow them to admit this out loud. So they decide to justify their behaviour by saying, "well, it wasn't my fault. They shouldn't have done this or said that." They mange to very neatly transfer that guilt to the other person.

The computer keeps recording it all but by now the other person isn't looking too good at all. Your computer, the sub conscious mind has recorded everything, often forming and recognizing familiar behaviour patterns. This can form a basis for what you will draw to you in any relationship until the pattern of behaviour is changed. What are you creating for you?

Of course the other person in this scenario feels hurt and emotionally battered. Perhaps they don't understand the degree of anger aimed at them. They feel emotionally whipped so they decide to withdraw into a silent world, thinking but not speaking. Communication becomes less and less, demonstrations of love become few and intimacy is either gone or loaded with aggression. If nothing is done to repair the relationship it will eventually break apart as each feels justified and each verbally hurts the other more and more. Sometimes at this point it's already too late to save the relationship. The war of words may have just gone too far.

But let's rewind a little. You began with a lot of love for this person. You gave them a commitment of your energy, your trust and your time. Sometimes a relationship doesn't stand the test of time. Sometimes you get together to end a behavioural pattern that has followed you for a number of lifetimes in a relationship with that particular person. On these occasions you always feel extremely drawn to the other person at the first meeting. You feel you already know them on a deep level. And you do. Your soul recognizes their soul. It's *soul recognition*.

You know now about the cave, cave flu and cave behaviour. Some responsibility is required of you. Recognition is 80%. It is your responsibility to decide what if any re-action you will use. Will you join the other person in a slanging match, or will you use the Stop sign? Time out. This is an excellent tool. It gives each one time to cool off, to think and to take control of their emotions. You can leave the room to give time for this. Even leaving for just a short time is very effective.

When you do come back into the room ask—what's the *real* reason? What's happening in your life? Where is all this anger *really* coming from? Communicate! Find out what's happening. There's always a reason. Often it's actually nothing to do with you. It's someone else, or a difficult situation at work or outside the home. Why do they take it out on you? Because somewhere in that computer of a mind they know you are the one they love and trust. It may be deep but it's there.

Because you are now aware you can prevent those large cracks occurring in your relationships. The buck stops with you. Especially now you have all this awareness and understanding. It's time to work out *why*. The person you love is still there but they may be living in the cave and hiding their love and those special qualities you enjoy.

Stop—Time Out—Evaluate—Communicate

Don't speculate! No matter how much you think you know the other person, you don't know everything that's happened to bring the other person to this point. They haven't told you yet. So stop. Go back and ask what's happened? What are the events? Coax them into opening up, to tell you, to explain. Then healing through love, through talking, can begin.

Sub Conscious Body Talk

The sub conscious mind continually sends messages to the body. Just like a computer it records everything and sends a message for your body to respond in a particular manner. This is great in a loving positive situation, not so good when someone's angry at you. You have the power to only acknowledge positive body talk. You have a choice. *Always there is choice.* Even if you forget and enter into cave language, you can still recognize where you've gone and say, "Hey, where am I? What am I doing? Stop." At any point you can do this. This also honours your commitment to the other person. You care enough to stop, to work it out, to listen and to talk. To root out the core reason for the anger. Actions really do speak louder than words. People will judge you by your actions. By saying stop and putting your hand up, you are saying I care about you. Your actions reflect your thinking. Your hand is saying stop! Your voice is saying stop! It's a very powerful message but sometimes it has to be.

Love is So Powerful

Love is very powerful too. As I've already said, love can lead us to feel we want to commit our lives to another. Or that we like a person as a brother, or a sister, and so form strong bonds of friendship. Love is not ambitious, competitive or spiteful. It is not infatuation. Infatuation fills a personal want or need. It doesn't last and usually departs in sadness. Unfortunately the attraction is fleeting and sometimes, just fills an inner need to feel loved, to realize you are still attractive to the opposite sex.

So how do you know love? Love is a harmonizing, uniting, deeply caring force. A very strong emotional energy. It is powerful enough to guide the Universe. When you love someone you want them to be all they can be. You support them in various ways. You allow them to grow emotionally as a person within the relationship. You encourage them with their goals, you are their trusted best friend, and you accept them as they are—warts and all because none of us are perfect. For love to grow and flourish you need to accept the person as they are. This forms a foundation of balance. True love is unconditional. It doesn't say, "I'll only love you if you do this or that." When you love someone you respect them as an individual. After all, we are all different. They may have an opinion that differs from yours. Love allows this and loves them anyway. You agree to disagree—and it's ok.

Love lasts because both parties are able to do this. They are able to work out their differences and to find middle ground to proceed on. They feed their love by continually communicating with each other verbally and physically. They have a mutual respect and when you respect someone you don't shout and abuse them, you just talk to them. Respect is very important in any relationship if it is to last. Love will grow and keep growing as each person continues to contribute to the relationship by nurturing it, communicating, caring and loving each other.

It's often said that love built on friendship will last. This is because friends talk a lot. They share the events of their day, their feelings, insecurities, upsets and victories. This is true communication. Events and experiences are given feelings, exposed in trust to the other; they feel secure with the other person. When love is added those feelings deepen.

Yet each one respects the other and each one remains an individual within the 'whole' of the relationship. So the relationship is able to move, to evolve and to grow stronger. Each one feels secure. A relationship is a growing energy. It moves with emotions and adjusts to outer events. This movement keeps the relationship alive. It never becomes a stagnant state. There is a comfortable security knowing you are loved as you are. It builds a confidence in yourself and in the relationship. You have no need to seek love elsewhere because you already have a special love. You feel satisfied deep within. You love another on any level of relationship because you <u>choose</u> to. You no longer <u>need</u> to.

Usually others will sense an 'air' about you. You may seem confidently happy, content, and secure. They wonder how they can be like this. It's not a secret. It's true love. It's working on that relationship, keeping it alive. It's an energy that must be fed and must be worked at.

You behave quite differently in a work situation when you feel secure. The feeling of security is very important even as a baby. As a baby you felt secure in your mother and fathers love. Your needs were always

147

met. You were cuddled, shown affection, encouraged to smile, to talk, to walk. Everything you needed to grow was encouraged with love.

You were given such praise when you succeeded. Your parents spent time with you because they wanted to, not because they had to. Your sub-conscious mind, the computer, received this message repeatedly. The feeling of being loved, of feeling secure was built stronger and stronger. You felt happy and responded joyfully to that unconditional love.

No matter how many times you spoke gibberish while learning to talk it didn't matter because you were continually encouraged to keep going and to keep trying. The many times you fell over while trying to take those first steps didn't matter. If you hurt yourself there were always lots of cuddles and kisses to make it better. As a baby when you got sick or you fell down, there was still great love for you. You were an individual yet totally dependent on another person. But that person is totally supporting you as you learn and grow in a loving environment. You felt secure and able to make mistakes. Yet they didn't matter because you were forever growing and learning. You need this unconditional love as an adult as well.

But sometimes you get to school and everything changes. You look for others to love you, even just a little. To help that along you might begin to seek other people's approval. Sometimes this grows out of proportion. Another's approval becomes vital. You begin to put your own needs aside. Love is powerful. You feel your parents unconditional isn't enough. You want more from this new environment. Often through peer pressure and dominance your perception of love can change. It is sad today that due to both parents being forced to go out to work to survive, a child often feels alone. There's really no one there to show them love, to listen. Parents no longer have the time.

So a child can easily feel they must conform to other's needs and wants just to be accepted. It becomes survival of the fittest at school. Be tough and dominant or be swallowed up. So the picture changes. Of course this isn't always the case, but too often it is today. The sub-conscious just keeps on recording new images so new responses are sent out to the body for a physical response. The Universe listens in as well.

Thirty Minutes a Day

Even if parents must work to survive it is vital they make a time available to communicate and listen to their child. Encourage that child to speak of the events of their day and how they feel about those events. To share the joys, upsets and achievements each day. You know just thirty minutes of undivided attention can make such a difference.

A child is very sensitive and picks up on negative comments very quickly. Talking prevents that 'weed' taking root. Talking gives them the tools to cope with life and other people with their varied personalities. And all it takes is thirty minutes a day.

The pictures formed in your sub conscious in childhood often stay with you as you enter adulthood and begin looking for a partner. You're looking for someone to love you, someone to share your secrets with, someone to feel secure with who accepts you just as you are.

At this point, with your new awareness and the tools provided in this book, you can work on changing the picture your sub conscious has formed about <u>you.</u> So you can begin to love yourself and stop looking outside of yourself for approval. Don't try to be somebody you're not because you believe this is how someone else wants you to be. Come back to you and love yourself first! Then you are able to love another in a balanced secure way. You can begin with these affirmations:

> **I accept myself totally
> with unconditional love**

> **I am worthy and secure
> within myself**

Chapter Eleven

Honouring Yourself

Ok, we have looked at the vital importance of communication, listening, commitment and love in a relationship. If you have been carrying this information over into your own relationships and doing a little honest reviewing, any adjustments or even over hauls will have become glaringly obvious to you. Doing this review step by step makes it achievable to be able to work on any adjustments needed so you *can* enjoy wonderful relationships.

You may be thinking that I'm only talking in terms of two—two friends, two lovers, or two workmates. But Master Kuthumi reminds you that you are the most important ingredient of all. Why is that? Could it be to ease your ego or make you feel good? No, of course not. It's because you have made a choice. You have decided you want to be better. You want to have a loving, peaceful relationship. One built with trust and openness. And so yes, you <u>are</u> most important because you made a very positive choice at this point in your life. It's a very positive step. One which has created great awareness in all relationships and interactions with others in your life. You will be more observant of another's words, reactions, body language and behaviour. You will be more aware of your own as well.

However it's all about tuning in to your feelings in an instant. This is also where your higher self kicks in, guiding you constantly through those feelings. What you feel and what you think is extremely important. These emotions must be acknowledged by you. No one else, just you. Your *sense* of self worth will depict just how much self worth you have. If you think this isn't very important, or you tell yourself, "I'm ok, I'm just too busy." That's a cop out! You're selling yourself short and covering up a low self esteem. You know, it's time to get greedy. Really greedy. It's time to spoil yourself and not feel guilty about it. It's time to think of all the good things you did today, right down to those tasks you completed at work. Time to think of you with no guilt! If that ego self tries to sneak in making you feel guilty then honour it by acknowledging yes it's there, leave my mind now, I have no need to feel guilty.

There are times you need to love and acknowledge you, and times to acknowledge others. But don't leave you out. It's important to honour yourself and you can do this in a number of ways. From buying something nice you really want just for you, having a long luxurious bath, giving yourself a pat on the back when you complete a job well. Acknowledge it. After all, wouldn't you comment if a workmate pointed out to you a job they had completed well? What makes you think you're any different? You're not! You deserve praise too so honour yourself.

As you grow and become more confident and happy in the person you are, there are things you just can't be bothered with. One of those can be replying to an angry person. Picture this, you're driving along a straight road, decide to turn, and signal. Half way through your turn off the road, there's a screech of brakes and the third car behind you hits the back of the car directly behind you. She has been inattentive and noticed brake lights too late. She hits the car in front of her. You carry on with your turn and park the car. She rushes over to you screaming and shouting. You open your mouth to speak but she over rides you and continues her accusations. She won't allow you to speak so you wind up your car window, signal, and drive off.

To be heard you would have to shout louder. Do you want to do this? You do have a choice. Always there is choice. Sometimes it is better to remain silent. This is honouring you also. You see that other person would love you to shout back, to feed *their* anger so they can retaliate some more. Why buy into their stuff? You don't have to. You don't *have* to reply.

Have you noticed in an argument replies give added ammunition? What may have begun as a disagreement on one thing now grows because another person really disagrees with your view point. Then you sometimes disagree back because ego has stepped in and neither of you can let the other 'win.' So each one gets louder and louder in an attempt to win and dominate the other using the other's responses. Sometimes it's better to be silent than to expel all that energy. You can say quietly," I disagree," and walk away til later when you have a better chance to talk logically and be listened to. Master Kuthumi speaks constantly of our emotional body and how we must overcome it and learn to become the observer. I have just given you a scenario of how to successfully achieve that. This builds self reliance. You understand so you are in control of your words and emotions.

You are able to listen, to be compassionate, yet remain confident in your own beliefs, your own understanding. You have no need to compete, manipulate or conform to the way someone else wishes you to be.

Have the courage to listen to that inner voice. Begin to trust your higher self. Learn to think, to be independent and solve your own problems via your higher self. If you occasionally fall over or make a mistake—so what? Every one does. You won't be the first or the last. Learn from it and keep moving forward.

Comparing is Wasted Energy

How often do you compare yourself with someone else? Be honest. Most people do at some stage. When you compare yourself constantly to another you are telling your sub conscious repeatedly, "I'm not good enough. They are better than me." Often this develops a self defeatist pattern where you never believe you will be good enough. You push yourself harder and harder physically working long hours to achieve. Know what? You never will. Because that's what you've repeatedly told yourself. "I'm not good enough." You fail to see your own successes because you won't let yourself acknowledge them. So you continue to self sabotage. This is why it is so important to honour yourself continually.

When you compare yourself to others you seek another's opinion to constantly validate how well you are doing. You give away your power—all of it! Far better to use your yard stick, your own thought process to accomplish what you wish to. This may help you. When you were a child and you did something wrong you were told you were bad. You were made to *feel* bad often by a form of punishment. However it wasn't you who was bad, it was what you _did_. It was the _action_ that was bad. Yet being told constantly *you* were bad created a low self esteem. I ask you to think on this for a time. Really think and see if this applies to you. If it does then it's being presented to you as an opportunity. An opportunity to make some changes within. To finally break the pattern formed as a child. Make the commitment to yourself and honour yourself in this way. It begins first with recognition, then making the commitment to implement change.

Change Is Everywhere

Change is part of our evolution and our DNA is changing. It seems our evolutionary change is inevitable. Our choice is in whether we agree to go with the flow and move forward in Grace, or whether you decide to resist and to hold on to old beliefs simply because they're there even though you've long outgrown them.

How many times do you do things the way you've always done them simply because that's the way it's always been done? Even if a better way is presented to you, you turn back to the old way. This is what you're being asked to do now. To look to a new way, a better way. To understand and to renew your faith as well.

In a way many have become a little like a robot. Not stopping to ask if what politicians are telling you is right or not. Or what anyone tells you. Most people are so busy they don't pause to stop and think, and to ask the question, "Is that right?" It's time to stop and to consider, is this _my_ truth? Or is it manipulation by someone else?

Trust in the Divine Order of the Universe

Do you still have faith in the Divine order of the Universe? Do you still have faith in God? Do you still trust your own judgement? Do you trust and believe in you?

You probably haven't thought too much about these things recently. Some people are just full of doom and gloom about our future. They want you to feel the same way which to them justifies their attitudes. But hang on a minute! Aren't they trying to give you the cave virus? Sounds like it to me. No way! Where's that Stop sign?

You need to align with your higher self. Connect to soul—your soul. Decide not to stay around people with the cave virus. Meditate, meditate, and meditate. I'm continually encouraging people to meditate. You know why? Because you can _feel_ the Divine energy. You can _feel_ that peace, that love. You can, it's so true. You **_can_** experience bliss! And afterwards those same feelings stay with you. You know this is real because you actually _felt_ it. You touched the energy of the Divine. Therefore in feeling this how can you not trust?

Your higher self, that small inner voice, is a part of Divine Consciousness within you. It's the voice that tells you, "Don't do that". You know this is not right." It keeps you on track, the right track, because it only wants the best for your highest good. And that's it! *You're* highest good. It's not about being number one, being Mr or Mrs perfect, pushing someone else aside to get the position, no it's not about any of that. You need to trust again. But not in someone else, trust yourself—your higher self.

The great Shift of the Ages that is happening on our planet right now. The beginning and ending of cycles. But man is such that he cannot go forward if he doesn't trust. Many are often driven by the ego through a need to control. To control situations and others. There is a lack of personal self discipline and the ego is able to push forward. Let me ask you, "How can you fulfil your life mission in this life time?"

To be guided by and to listen to your higher self takes great courage. Yet this is your mission! This is what your higher self wishes you to achieve. To overcome and to understand the ego self. To work in the Light and trust.

When you have a lack of self love it is very difficult to give to others. You easily become selfish, jealous of others and resentful. Ego will feed on the emotional thoughts and feelings. This can bind you in endless cycles of negative behaviour. This actually happens quite a lot. You may say, "Oh, that's just the way it is." Is it? Or is it that you can't be bothered to make a change?

You can turn on the Light any time you choose to. But looking around it seems many have forgotten that they can. The ego has them so tied up in the material world wanting more and more, they really have lost their way. Yet it's still there, still waiting, still shining brightly. Isn't that wonderful? That's real unconditional love!

Whatever you have done, or do, that Light is still there, waiting, with no judgement what so ever. It's sad that man is so used to negative patterns of egotistical behaviour he often mistrusts and simply can't believe he's good enough.

> **There is no judgment as powerful as the judgement you give yourself.**

Many continually think they have to be better than they are. Yet unconditional love accepts them as they are right now, warts and all. Why is it they are unable to just let go and accept themselves? This greatly inhibits growth on all levels. It binds them in darkness. Please remember this—write it out—

Higher vibrations transform lower vibrations.

The more Light quotient you are holding the faster this process will be. The more Light you hold the faster you will process sadness and loss. It will be transformed.

On the Other Side

On the other side there is no time. The other side is filled with Light essence. Therefore the Light is not ruled by Earth (Linear) time. When you meditate you are often surprised how much linear time has gone by. That's because you visited the other side where time does not exist. The same occurs when you day dream. Again you are visiting a dimension on the other side, even though your physical body remains in our world. You are multi-dimensional! Both of these experiences are proof of that.

By living fully in the Light energy you will create a new life. Your new Earth. When you work in this Light, live and think in the Light, your old thought patterns and behaviours are transformed. Your DNA changes, your cells change, your magnetic vibrational energy changes. The more Light energy you hold the faster and greater the changes. Your conscious levels also transform as these changes align within you. Your auric field also aligns with the Light.

We previously spoke of confusion. Many people today would say they are confused. You read and hear about energy and a new Earth, about creating and manifesting, yet the physical world does not change. It remains the same. Many continue to go in circles, chasing financial gains in long hours of slave labour. They are really unable to enjoy their work because they're too focused on just doing it!

So many feel confused. Why is this? It's because some have lost trust and faith. Their thoughts are not strong enough in faith and the Light quotient is not strong enough within them to sustain a higher dimensional existence. They continually search outside of themselves. As long as mankind continues to do this, he will not reach his destination of Light.

Master Kuthumi Speaks on Behavioural Patterns

You see it comes back to you, to being all you can be. It is there for you, it always has been. It is a journey of exploration of your senses, emotions, and behavioural experiences. There is a doorway in front of you leading you through a portal to a higher dimension, a higher vibration.

This chapter concerns relationships and has covered some behavioural patterns. It is hoped this has given you a greater understanding regarding the choices available to you. What you see outwardly presented to you daily are in many cases another's fears, insecurities, and lack of knowledge. So they speak to control a situation or worse, you. Through this book and your life journey so far, you are able to understand this. You have taken personal responsibility and indeed some have made huge steps forward in their lives. This is to be commended.

Now we take a step further in spirit and Light. We have given you much to ponder on. When you have made your choices, I urge you to think of your actions, that which supports your thoughts and emotions, your goals also and your dreams. We here see many goals and dreams and wishes blow away and leave, just as the wind blows away the leaves on a tree in autumn. There is nothing to stop that happening you see. There has been no action taken to anchor the leaves, just as sometimes there has been no action to anchor or create and so bring a wish or dream into being.

This is where mankind is now. Bringing the Light energy into your reality. To anchor that energy in your thoughts, actions and your world. To live and flow in that Light energy. To let go of old ways. Yet to let go requires trust does it not? It is time for you now to trust in your self, to trust in your own core truths which you have created, those you hold within you. Only then can you trust in God's Light and truly live and breathe in a new way.

I am Kuthumi

Chapter Twelve

The Kingdom Of Heaven Is Within You

So we've talked about honouring your self. How important that whole issue is. Because it is a big one. It's not just about saying, "Oh, ok yes I'll buy that skirt for myself." It's much more than that and expands to far deeper levels. It's really about loving and respecting yourself and that includes your opinions, your time, your actions, and also honouring your body. What Kuthumi refers to as your template. You could say it's about minding your own business because you need to begin to listen to your own inner guidance.

The Three Minds

So let's look a little more closely at you. We've talked about your three minds—the conscious mind, the sub-conscious mind and the super conscious mind.

The conscious mind deals with daily decisions, emotions, and the thoughts in both the left and right side of the brain.

The sub-conscious mind is the computer. It stores information, feelings, and experiences. It doesn't have feelings as such, but it does react to certain situations which it remembers. These situations would be comments or actions that are repeated a number of times. The computer records all of these from the time you drew your first breathe. It carries on recording until you take your final breathe and your soul returns to the soul plane once more and you greet your soul family.

The super conscious mind is linked to your higher self, to soul, to the Divine. Through this process your own intuition and spiritual 'gifts' are brought forward.

All of these make up the wondrous being you are, dressed in a human overcoat. At the beginning we told you everything including you, is energy. Whatever energetic thoughts you repeatedly feed your mind the Universe will bring to you and this will create your own outer reality. This amazing organ called a brain, with all its electrical pulses, is able to bring to you everything required to create what you desire of a higher nature because it is able to speak a Universal language.

There are vast electromagnetic forces throughout our Universe. Scientists know this. This force controls our Sun, our gravity field and the Universal Laws. You also carry an electromagnetic field around and within you. Blood is your greatest conductor of electricity. Electricity is magnetic. It is these combined forces from your body and the Universe which carry that energy, capable of holding your very thought imprints throughout your body via your nervous system—in an instant of Linear time.

If you are in fear of a situation that is only *likely* to happen, but you convince yourself it will happen, this energy travels throughout your body building anxiety and stress around all your major organs. Your cells begin to jump around like jelly beans, which creates some of that 'tummy doing summersaults' feeling. From there, your entire body is reacting to your initial worrying thought. Your sub-conscious mind records it as something you wish to happen, so it proceeds to use the Universal energy force to draw it to you. It is after all, only obeying your wishes. Like attracts like. The sub-conscious mind is unable to think, therefore cannot differentiate between positive and negative. It is a slave really. Whatever your constant repetitive thoughts are, whether that is lack of work, money, friends, success or fear of illness, those thought waves travel out through the Ethers of the Universe. Those magnetic waves of energy will seek out, attract and combine with others to bring your desire into being. Know that thought imprints are extremely powerful.

Man is such that he often worries and focuses on the negatives in his life. You may be thinking for a while that nothing's going right today, everything I try goes wrong, I'm going to be late, someone took my park, and on and on, all negative thoughts—have you noticed? Yet I think everyone can relate to them. Add these few thought s to your other dominant thoughts today, tomorrow, next week and you begin to see what's happening here. Usually you don't even think of your thoughts this way. You may think it's just another day. Well, like attracts like!

Many people say," Yes, I want success, yes I want to be rich, yes I want to be debt free." They then fret and worry constantly when a bill arrives in the post, or the groceries cost more and there's little money left in the budget. What do you do? Most will produce volumes of thought around lack. Because when you worry about lack of money it is in itself a powerful form of lack. Even saying, "I need more money," translates to financial lack on your thought imprint. Did you realize that every negative thought dramatically reduces your own electromagnetic power? With enough negative thoughts your mental state will reduce to a state of depression. The physical body will often become quite weak, tired, with little vital energy. But this doesn't have to be. It is you who decides if you will or will not experience these states of being. Please, think about this.

The Super-Consciousness

The higher mind has various names; some call it the Super Consciousness, others the transitional power or the Universal mind. These names all link to 'I Am', the Divine consciousness of God, the Source. It is referred to in the Bible through Moses when a voice 'spoke' to him from a burning bush. Think of this for a moment. I believe there are many examples regarding this in the Bible. Some have been removed by those who didn't understand and operated perhaps on a lower vibrational level.

But as I said, think for a moment. A burning bush. Would you listen? Would you run? Would you respond and if so, how would you respond? Of course Moses did respond, he stopped and acknowledged the voice seemingly coming from a bush on fire. Was this a test of faith for Moses? In any event upon his positive response Moses was shown how to lead the tribes out of the desert to freedom.

This knowledge has always been available. Jesus often went up to Mt Sinai to pray and often came back with powerful higher mind imprints of what he should do next. He was being divinely guided and without question was connecting and communicating with God. Jesus so easily slipped into the higher vibration required as Jesus was a messenger of God; therefore he held a great Light quotient. It was opened and expanded upon his 'baptism.' That was when Jesus opened and accepted his higher powers of clairvoyance, clairaudience, and of course his great healing powers. So great was his connection he seemingly created miracles. This was his soul journey for the short time he was on Earth. Look at the great example he left. Over 2000 years later man is finally beginning to get it!

Many millions today around the world connect to God's energy through their own Super Conscious mind. This is done by working with a higher, finer energy. You can see it as Light—white Light— part of God's outer energy field. We know it exists. We know it is real. We feel it. We know it contains unimagined potential and it's freely available to all mankind. It has the power to give us higher guidance, hope, healing and enables us to create a new Earth and a better way of life.

Many famous people have connected to this energy. Look at the absolute strength of Joan of Arc. What an example of faith, particularly when she was imprisoned for her beliefs! Many experience a form of persecution today as they step onto their spiritual path and begin a new relationship with their spiritual guides and spirit. This is called connecting to the power within. To connect to this great and infinite power you must first learn to quieten your conscious mind. This can be quite difficult for some, especially if fear or control are issues. This is where the ego often plays as well. Yet although this may seem to be a difficult task, it can be achieved and indeed has been by millions and millions of people who are all experiencing this wonderful journey.

A Test of Faith

Perhaps it's meant to be this way to allow us the opportunity to pause, to reflect, heal and let go of our past which can be so difficult. As you step onto your path, your faith is tested also.

Perhaps you want to go to a meditation, but are often faced with the disapproval of loved ones. This can be scary, but you are not alone. Your spirit guides are always with you helping you to trust your inner feelings, your 'vibes' and learning to be still to enter a very quiet space where your soul resides. Your guides relay messages through the Super Conscious mind. You receive it as a feeling, a message or a vision. This is a place where you must learn absolute trust. It is not yours to question why or how. This is especially important if you give any messages to others. You are only the messenger after all. You must trust your inner voice completely. In doing this you also develop strength. As you listen more and more to your own inner voice you trust more and hear more clearly. You become very receptive to the messages from your higher self with practice.

Your higher self will never tell you a lie. By contrast the conscious mind can and does. You have to be alert. It is your higher self that always shows you the path for your highest good. As you seek a path of fulfilment, your thoughts and wishes go out to the Universe. That thought energy seeks a magnetic force to empower your thought imprints and bring to you that which you desire. For example, let's say you have a strong inner desire to be a healer. In your mind's eye you see your healing room, what it looks like, you see yourself healing someone. The image is growing. It's becoming quite embellished. Your sub-conscious remembers all these details and seeks out similar forces and situations to bring you that desire through magnetic force. As your faith and trust in yourself grows you may begin to seek out healing classes and classes of higher learning. You just *feel* you need to do this. It's all part of your inner desire. Your higher self is pushing you forward to begin your higher journey. It's what *you* chose. Very probably even before you incarnated which is another reason why you feel so drawn to become a healer. As you feel more and more fulfilled you look for more learning, more knowledge and higher understanding.

Whatever your inner dream is that repeatedly enters your creative mind the Universe will bring situations to you in order for that to become a reality. Focus is the key. Do not waver. Do not doubt yourself. Believe. You need an unwavering faith to bring you your desire and to enable you to fulfil your soul contract to humanity.

At this time in man's revolution, we must work harder than ever. If we are to succeed and progress to a higher level you need to throw out completely all thoughts of lack on any level. That means physical, mental, emotional and spiritual levels. Delete all thoughts of lack. You see you don't need them any more. They're obsolete. Outdated. They only remain because you keep giving them the 'kiss of life' through your thought process in the conscious mind.

Albert Einstein said,
"More important than thought is imagination."

The majority of people in the world haven't got this yet. Many are too busy working long hours, paying bills and worrying. Cave language. Stop! Take some time to dream. There is great power in this as we've already discussed.

The Seasons of Life

Our world has seasons. Autumn is a time of finishing off projects and preparing for the winter season. There is time to be still in winter. Spring gives you time to prepare and plant seeds of promise. Summer is a time to reap what you have sown. Mankind is in a summer season now. We are reaping what we have sown. Person by person, country by country. What have you sown? Is it what you truly desire? We all have the creative power within us to write a new script for ourselves. The first step is to ask what it is you desire. If you have done the inner work and formed a good relationship with yourself you are on the right path.

Your will power resides in your conscious mind. Also the ego plays it's whims out there as well. Those who have a strong will often endured a difficult path in youth. However as they grew in wisdom they learnt to harness the power of their will and to use it to convert their dreams into reality. In youth there is often much impulsive behaviour. This combined with a strong will can lead to difficulty, yet can also provide the greatest opportunities for learning. The most difficult lessons are so often the ones you never forget and they are the most valuable.

The conscious mind will often deceive you. Sometimes you don't see a situation clearly or as it actually is. Sometimes you choose to see what you want to see. This can lead to disillusionment. Through this you imprint anxiety, worry, poverty and false hope into your sub-conscious mind which of course merely obeys the imprint and brings you the situation you have asked for through the imprint.

So you see how it all works? You see also perhaps how all of those old habits are now holding you back. The Light particles you connect to around you are powerful. However if you add the Light of God through the super-conscious mind, then your creation is limitless, just as it is with God.

The Right Diamond Key

There is one other important key however. If you are on a 'fast track,' and don't really connect to your own inner truth and Light then the Light will be dimmed considerably. The Light cannot be misused. So no short cuts allowed! The key is connecting to your own Diamond Light. The higher heart link to your soul. When you are connected you are in a right relationship, as above—so below. You feel joy, an incredible joy. Many who feel this God Light energy for the first time, weep.

This energy is slightly different to the energy you connect to when you begin to meditate. You need to go higher to connect to the God Light energy. The higher you go the more Light energy you receive. You receive this from a higher dimension where time does not exist. Therefore when you are able to hold this energy within you are able to process your emotions very quickly. This is due to the higher vibration you now carry and also your higher awareness.

At this point you are very aware of the various dimensions of Spirit, the energy levels, soul and the illusions which man has created and continues to create. All of this knowledge provides a deeper relationship with yourself. Do you now begin to understand how important this is? Do not doubt yourself as a person. You are able to function and achieve your goals step by step. Respect yourself and your own opinion.

As you begin to connect and work through the super-conscious mind and higher self you will clearly see the games people play. You will see when their ego is in action. When they are angry, demanding or putting you down, when they not being nice—this is all ego in action. Recognize this. Remember 80% is recognition. This recognition gives you a split second pause to click to another vibration, to check your own ego in place and not go into retaliation mode. That's why that split second recognition time is so important. It gives you that moment, that precious moment to enable you to stay in your own power—your higher power.

Everyone does have that spark of Diamond Light within, even the meanest person you can imagine. However those mean ones are blocking it off with their strong will and negative intent. When you remember this it helps you to deal with them in a correct manner. Because you now see the game. You see the front they are projecting while hiding their own inadequacies and insecurities. You see it and it's a game, a play.

Once you recognize this it puts everything into a new light (if you pardon the pun.) You get and are able to maintain a new perspective on other people. You understand far more. You are seeing from your higher self. You lose the fear. Maybe you've been carrying some form of fear around for years. You've been told you don't need it but never fully understood. Suddenly now you do. Now you see. So you begin a new relationship with your higher self. Thoughts release and change. Feelings lift. A new way begins within!

Chapter Thirteen

A New Beginning

Let's pause for a moment of reflection. I want to ask you how you're getting on with your relationships? They should be easier to handle now, easier to understand and easier to go into another headspace until the heat dies down and you have a chance to assimilate what is really important. What really is the issue and is this their stuff or yours? This last part is important. It's a big part of your transition to a new you.

Is it Your Stuff, or Theirs?

So how do you tell if it's their stuff or yours? Simple. Ask yourself how you feel. Be honest. If you're angry or have a strong negative emotion then it's your stuff and you need to sit and ask yourself why you feel this way. Because that person is mirroring an aspect of your attitude and behaviour that you just didn't want to see. No matter how hard it is you really need to stay with this one until you are honest with yourself and feel you have found the reason within your self for your emotional response. That aspect may be deep within you, but it's there. That other person you're so angry at is playing a part in order to bring this issue to your attention to deal with. So the more emotion you feel, the more you may react by reliving and replaying what happened.

You may ask," Well why do I want to do this. It sounds like a lot of work." The answer is this. As the person stands there and makes you react in anger, indignation etc, they are mirroring you. Yes. They are showing you exactly what you do. They are showing you how others see you in that same aspect of behaviour. The 'mirror' is showing you. No one really likes to see this or admit it either. But I can tell you the 'mirror' of behaviour will keep being presented to you until you are ready to stop and do some inner work. To perhaps admit yes, I *can* do this. I need to delete this behaviour. Remember that person is playing their part in showing you. Sometimes the person that irritates you the most or you most dislike is your biggest teacher sent from Spirit. So the sooner you recognize and acknowledge the behaviour pattern the sooner you can move on and leave that aspect of you behind. You are really fine tuning your attitude and becoming a better person. A more enriched soul.

Now it may be you like to always be in control. You can say," I've always been this way." That's ok, it's just that you've got a bit out of balance and that aspect of you has become too strong and too dominant. But it can be adjusted. Perhaps if this is you it's time to realize that you can't control every person and every situation. Neither do you like being told what to do. That's the 'mirror' at work.

This is one way the Universe teaches us and helps us to learn, while bringing us back to balance. Recognition is 80%. You have to be totally honest with yourself.

And there's no point in holding anger within. If you do you are binding yourself in chains. Those chains will have to be undone sooner or later. It'll be worse if you feed that anger by adding more anger. Oh dear, getting to bit of a block now, maybe entering victim mode. Ouch! As I said those chains will have to be undone in this life or another. OOOHHH! Don't want to create that. Oh no!

Deal with your emotions now and try not to stew and rehash old happenings. We live in a time of personal responsibility. That means looking after your physical, mental and emotional selves. Your totality. Let go. Bash a pillow, a ball, exercise, whatever you need to do to release that negative energy and anger. Then you begin the cleansing and the healing. You overcome it. How great is that?

Most people have something to dig out and to clear and to heal from. Some are big issues, some small. Size doesn't matter here. Healing does. Where's your CAN DO button? Put up that STOP sign. Get out the cave ladder. Begin! Deal with your old baggage and get rid of it! All the tools in this book can help you to get the job done. Master Kuthumi gives you this affirmation:

> **I am worth it**
> **I am a beautiful person**
> **I allow my Light to shine.**

Say this one often. Write it out and put it everywhere where you'll see it often. On the fridge, the bathroom mirror, the computer screen, the desk. Everywhere. It's one that will help you a great deal to move forward with confidence. Every one has an inner gift—every one. It's just that some people can't see it, or choose not to. I think this is sad because what they're saying is, "I'm not worthy." You didn't come into this world feeling like that. You were shown or told over and over until it became an imprint and you eventually believed it.

Let me ask you, "Do you still want to believe it?" Because if you do then I can't help you. No one can. Because you are still choosing to believe it as a core truth. You can say as many affirmations as you like but they won't change anything. Why? Because you are still choosing to hold on to your core truth that you're not worthy. Until you are ready to make a change, nothing will change. So you see it really is up to you isn't it? It is up to you to choose what you will take on board and accept about yourself.

But know it *can* be changed. Either through your own recognition, your own choice, or by a great upheaval in your life. Sometimes—I said sometimes—your greatest change occurs through adversity in your life. All the crutches are taken away. You are forced to look at yourself and your life with brutal honesty. Out of necessity you make decisions for change because you have to.

Remember any old paradigm can be altered. You have the power within you. You now have the tools. It's not easy; no one said it would be. But the gold at the end of the path is so worth it. That gold is a new you! A better, happier you.

At the beginning we looked at your foundation. You forced out old 'blocks' that you no longer needed, that you felt you had long out grown, had not thought about. You did the maintenance and put some new 'blocks' in place to make you stronger and to give you a solid foundation. Now is perhaps your first test on how strong that foundation is that you built back then. If you haven't done enough admit it. Go back to the beginning of this book and do the exercises again. It's never too late. The important thing is that you admitted "I want to be better. I want happiness and abundance in my life. I deserve it." If you didn't need to revisit, then well done. You must be feeling great reading this now.

Failure—Is It Though?

I want to mention this because I think that at some point we all think this. How many times do you say," I can't, or I'm a failure, or I'm not good enough to do that." I'm here to tell you that you're selling yourself short. You are so much more—much more. Get out of the cave and see yourself doing it. Whatever it is. Have a go.

Know it's an experience, a learning. So what if you don't pass. Is it really so important. No. Only perhaps to you and what does that tell you? It's not really failure its experience. For better or worse it's just an experience. If it ends up a worse experience then learn from it but don't repeat it. Even that's a learning you know. And yes, I've said this before but this is a reminder. It's very important hence, the repeat.

Let's look now at worry. When you worry, you are either projecting a scenario about the past or the future. If it's the past it's already been played out. For better or worse it's happened. It cannot be changed and no amount of worry will change it. As I said the best scenario is that you learn from it. And the future? Well, what it really is, is a lot of if's and buts. A fantasy. Imagination. It hasn't happened and may not, unless you will it into being. And you can if you focus on a probable situation strong enough and long enough. It's called manifestation. But we're looking at worrying, so more likely it's a lot of ifs and buts. This is also when fear is likely to step into the picture as well. So what do you do? Find that STOP sign. And once again, you choose.

You will probably need some self discipline as you catch yourself worrying again. You need to turn it around and project a happy outcome to everyone's highest good. Begin living in the present. Not yesterday or tomorrow. Not in fear either. Because fear is an illusion. Fear usually comes from the mind. It's created. Visualize Light. Let that Light provide you with inner strength to endure and to overcome. In the pure Light no one can harm you.

You have the power to create what you desire, either physically, or mentally. You simply need to focus on that desire. You are able to change old behaviour, to change an imprint on the unconscious mind. You are capable and able to do these things. If you have followed this book and used the tools provided, you will know you can change. It is you who chooses what you will be, what you will experience, not another. It's very important to banish self doubt. Self doubt belongs in the cave. You will find if you choose to give energy to negative thoughts and self doubt you will be launched into the cave. The more self doubt you give energy to the deeper you will go. But make no mistake, <u>you</u> chose to go there.

Now I realize there are times when all of us will stand at the entrance to the cave. However it is up to each one of us to choose whether to enter or to leave. That's your choice.

21 Days to Change

During your transitional period make yourself the number one priority. It takes 21 days to change a habit. Be gentle yet focused on yourself. Don't allow yourself to be distracted. Focus on what you want to move forward from. It may be a behavioural pattern, an old hurt, something you still feel is a past mistake. Don't keep giving it energy. Don't keep feeding it. Time to let it go. You have the tools and you now have the awareness to do it. Allow yourself the compassion and the time to create change, to create your desire and your new life.

Do you Self Sabotage?

There is one other thing to look out for—self sabotage. You know sometimes you have all the best intentions in the world. You are sure you've made your mind up and you want to do it. You know you can. Then along comes the first hurdle. Suddenly your resolve wobbles, and then crumbles. You go back to old behaviour and before you know it you self sabotage yourself. Now you feel so bad. Worse than before. You reaffirm yourself as a failure. You enter the cave. STOP!

So you slipped up. Be kind to yourself. Every person who has ever gone on a diet has slipped up at some point. So what? Don't be so arrogant as to think you're the only person that's slipped up. Of course you're not. But you know it's not the slipping up that matters. It's the action you choose to take. That's where the learning is, that's where your growth is. Your action.

There are two paths here which you can choose. One path is to admit, ok, I mucked up. No big deal. Just start again and move forward. The other path is the cave, isolation, despair, pulling yourself down. Which path will you choose to take? You need to decide now, to prepare. Hopefully you will not have to choose. But, if you do, then you'll be prepared.

Turn To Success in Life

Everyone wants success. Most think it's only available to the few. Not true. It's there for all who want it. What does success mean to you? Some think of success as having money, expensive cars, maybe a big house. Others think of success as enjoy a sense of power in the community. Still others may feel success is enjoying a peaceful life of happiness having their basic needs met without too much bother. Some see success through their work, using all their energy to appear to be successful in their field so their peers can see just what height they've aspired to. As you can see success means different things to different people. So again, what does success mean to you?

This is a question which usually takes a little time to answer. It requires you to look deep within. Do you see success by your own standards or another's? What would God look on as success for you? Mmmm, lots of issues to ponder here. I'm going to look at a common one which is judging your success by another's standards. This may represent your boss to you. It's all about what *he* wants. So therefore, it's *his* success, not yours. Your reward is that you may be acknowledged and deemed to be successful. But by who's standard, and who's choice?

Another scenario may be in a larger organization. You may wish to seem better than another for various reasons. You might wish to be seen as doing more, being in front of the pack as it where. Some will extend a lot of energy in order to create this making themselves exhausted in the process, not just physically, but mentally also as they plan and create new strategies to get ahead and to be seen as successful. Yet all of this is *their* interpretation of success. It lies on the outer spheres of their life. They feel it's the only way and so try harder and harder to reach the top—to win. It's a very physical aspect.

But it is all an illusion which you create. What you really should be looking at is your inner world. Utilizing the Light energy, not looking at another with the eyes of judgement, but with eyes of compassion and understanding. Ok, maybe they haven't got it yet. Does that make them your enemy? The world is a beautiful place to be. Seeing through a man made illusion of material success *is* success to me.

You may say we have to live. Society is such that we have to make a living. That is true. But that can be done simply. It need not only be on a grand scale. Many think that *only* when they have expensive material possessions they are successful. They will be happy. But can they be sure of that? Whose standards of success are they using? It's really quite a question isn't it?

Success can also be measured through your passion. That one thing you create and do which makes you feel alive, joyful, and content. That one thing where you feel time stands still, where you simply are and you're filled with happiness. When you feel like this you know you have found your passion. It's what you are meant to be doing. Your higher self will be happy and that will flow through all of your being. You've just discovered God's vision of success for you.

Find Your Passion in Life

You find passion in your life by doing the things you love, and then narrowing it down to those few things that not only make you happy, but also give you joy. Then you narrow it down again to the one thing that completely fills you with a feeling of euphoria. <u>That</u> is your passion. It's what you came to share with mankind. You just know it, you feel it so you create it and share it. You feel bliss. Linear time stands still because you are working on another dimension. Your soul rejoices. Your passion is your ultimate success. Everything else is merely an illusion.

Chapter Fourteen

Tools for Transformation

The Light Rays

Previously we discussed how to distinguish what was your issue and what was not. I then went on to give you essential tools to cope with various situations including self sabotage, which is always a deep issue.

> **What you perceive you will project—in your words, attitude and actions**

The inner reflects the outer. This is none more true than in reflecting how you feel about yourself and how you see yourself. So it has been very important as you've worked through these chapters to do the inner work. Certainly you will feel stronger and more positive in your entirety. It is how you perceive you, your work and your place in this world of transformation and mixed energies. At this point you are taking full responsibility for your words, your actions, and your life. For many this can be difficult but why is this so? Because they find the responsibility difficult to maintain. It's often easier to roll along allowing others to shape your moods and to blame others for your problems.

It is easier to gossip and complain at the coffee machine than to step forward and create your reality in daily life. It's not too long before you become a cave dweller! Your thoughts, feelings and reactions all depend on others. Usually the boss, someone else at work or a friend.

It's so easy to blame someone else for all the wrongs in your life. You probably seek sympathy from others thinking you will feel better. This just sends you deeper into the cave.

We've discussed this and by now you know about cave language and behaviour, even the cave virus! You also know that the answer isn't outside of you or with someone else. It's within you! After all it was your own thoughts and actions that sent you to the cave in the first place. It was the reaction *you* chose. It's important to remind yourself of this because sometimes you forget and get caught up in someone else's creation. You catch the dreaded cave virus. If you remember to acknowledge to yourself, "Well, I put myself here," and in acknowledging that you are also saying, "I don't have to stay here."

How to Use the Rays of Spirit

Before we leave this I want to give you one other important tool to help you move forward when you find yourself in any of these situations. Often you know what you want in your life but others around you may not be so positive. That special tool is the Light. What is the Light? The Light is a form of energy from the God/Source. It's all around us but often we don't realize it or think about it. It's ours to use, to transform and uplift us. You can use the Light in any situation at all. Since we've been discussing surviving at work or with other people, let's continue to use these common examples. Here's a super easy method to connect to the Rays of Spirit.

The Ray of Love quick Meditation

To connect to the Ray of Love simply close your eyes and completely relax the physical body as we've done on previous meditations in this book.

Breathe deeply in and out three times to relax and align your subtle bodies.

Now breathe quietly. Completely relax your physical body.

Visualize a soft pink balloon. See that pink balloon as soft and full.

Now visualize the balloon moving closer to you until you seem to be inside the beautiful balloon, completely surrounded in the pink essence.

You feel safe, secure, loved inside the balloon. There is no fear at all.

Allow the essence of the pink Ray of Love energy to flow around and through you, softly energizing every cell in your body with Universal love.

You feel so calm, completely at peace.

Just stay in the pink Ray of Love balloon as long as you feel you need to because this Ray is transforming your perception of the situation and of you. It's lovingly lifting you up high in pure unconditional love. You will feel different. You will feel uplifted somehow.

Ask the Ray of Love to stay with you and surround you.

See yourself with the white pyramid of Light surrounding you and staying with you to protect you.

Now open your eyes and come back to the present.

You can use this simple technique as often as you need to in various situations. It's short, simple and effective. Best of all, it's free. How good does it get? If you're having trouble getting rid of that final little bit of negativity, use the soft pink balloon technique. You can also use it any time you need to feel some warm fuzziness and inner peace. Really!

But it doesn't stop there. You can use other rays as well. In today's busy world we are moving so fast you sometimes neglect your own temple—your body. You get physically ill with a cold or the flu as your body cries out for rest. If this is you, you won't feel like doing too much. This meditation only takes a few minutes, but remember intent is all when working with the higher energies.

The Ray of Healing quick Meditation

Find your self a relaxing place, a chair or a bed.

Again close your eyes. Relax your mind and your physical body as in previous meditations.

Breathe deeply in and out three times to relax and align your subtle bodies.

Breathe quietly.

Visualize now a pale blue healing balloon. I've always associated this with the Christ energy and this knowledge is the intent I use.

Visualize the pale blue balloon getting larger and larger. You feel very relaxed and calm.

You are soon encompassed in the pale blue healing balloon. The energy surrounds and fills you in your totality.

Now visualize circles of the pale blue Ray of Healing within the balloon moving slowly up and down your body, healing, cleansing.

Open yourself to accept the healing energy.

Now just sit quietly in the pale blue Ray of Healing balloon.

When you're ready, open your eyes.

Now ask for a white pyramid to surround you, to stay with you and protect you. Know it is so.

The healing energy will filter through your auric field including the mental and emotional bodies and finally through to the physical body soothing and healing as the energy moves around you.

This is how the Light Rays work. They are minuet particles of high and very powerful energy. They cannot be used for a negative intent. The Rays have always been available to us. Man has not fully understood how to utilize them.

The Violet Ray of Transformation Meditation

Here is another very simple visualization for transforming old negative thought patterns and behaviour. This can be yours or someone else's you picked up along the way.

Again, sit quietly and close your eyes.

Completely relax as before using the three breath method. Ensure your mind and physical body are totally relaxed.

Now visualize a beautiful violet coloured balloon.
See it getting larger and larger.

Once more visualize yourself safely inside the balloon surrounded in the Violet Ray essence.

Now repeat:

I now transform all negative thoughts and feelings into the Violet Ray. I no longer need any form of negativity in my life. I am Blessed in the Violet Ray process.

Stay a moment longer in the violet balloon allowing your new intent to fully manifest within. Know all negativity has been transformed into the Light. It is released from you.

Again, feel the complete peace and upliftment.

When you're ready, step out of the violet balloon and ask for a white pyramid to surround you, to stay with you and protect you. Know it is so.

There are times when each of us need help to step back onto our higher path. This Ray of Transformation is invaluable in reminding us, and bringing us back into balance again.

This next one is important in our times of transition on Earth right now. I really find this a big help when I feel stuck on a personal issue. Any channel will tell you, the more personal a decision is; the harder it is to hear spirit clearly. Believe me; this does it, every time.

The Ray of Clarity Meditation

Once more sit quietly. Close your eyes. Completely relax.

Still your physical body and mind. Just allow any busy thoughts to leave your mind. Sending persistent thoughts away on a leaf often helps. Visualize each persistent thought being carried away on a leaf until they are gone.

Again, breathe very deeply in and out three times as before. Feel the subtle shift.

Now visualize an aqua coloured balloon. This combines the colours of green and blue. It is a powerful colour which opens your higher heart, sending you the Ray of Clarity.

Visualize the aqua balloon getting larger and larger until it encompasses you, gently, lovingly.

Feel such peace. A stillness as your higher heart is activated through your Thymus to your Higher Heart. This is so special.

Now quietly, in your higher mind space, gently ask your question. As simply and clearly as possible.

Just sit quietly. Don't try to imagine scenarios. Wait to hear or be shown, or just to feel your answer. Be patient if this is your first time asking. You may need to practice a few times to be able to completely release your conscious mind.

Now feel the aqua Ray of Clarity filling your mental and emotional bodies. Simply be in that essence. Allow. Give yourself permission just to be.

When you feel you're finished, gently give thanks and step out of the aqua balloon.

Ask for a white pyramid to surround you, to stay with you and protect you. Know it is so.

Now open your eyes.

If you received any message it is best to write it down quickly. Once you get the hang of this it really is a great tool to use. Let's give you one more.

The Ray of Divine Peace

This ray is a peach colour which combines the higher colour rays of the Divine which is gold and the pink Ray of Love. Let's begin again.

Once more sit or lie quietly, close your eyes and relax. It's very important to trust and completely release your mind and physical body.

Breathe the three deep breathes in and out again. It's so important to completely fill up your lungs with air before releasing slowly through the mouth.

Visualize a peach coloured balloon. See it soft and full. Feel the Divinity of this balloon as your intent tells the Universe the highest essence Ray is being called upon.

See yourself surrounded in the peach colour as you fully and quietly absorb the very high essence of the Divine Ray.

Absorb, feel yourself surrounded in Divine peace. (If you begin to feel dizzy or your tummy starts doing summersaults, gently pull out and open your eyes.) You need more practice to feel the higher energies, that's all. Your physical body has to adjust.)

When you feel you have had your fill, give thanks and gently, oh so gently and slowly return to awareness. Ask the Ray of Divine Peace stay with you, surrounded in white Light. Know it is so. Now open your eyes.

You will certainly feel a difference using this ray. It's a beautiful energy to experience. There are many other Rays as well, but I feel these will serve you well at this point.

Simplify Your Life

This is one of Master Kuthumi's favourite sayings. Looking around I can see why. He has repeated this message in his teachings for a long time. We can no longer live on endless credit or beyond your means. And yes, it has been so easy to obtain credit. A situation now being addressed on a global scale. Yet here we are. Taking responsibility, boldly stepping forward and creating a new world. You may have a lot of debris from past mistakes as you see it. Of course, there are no mistakes, only learning experiences.

You may be struggling trying to release old energies and go to work each day. Sometimes past baggage holds onto you like glue. You know you should move on, but somehow it's just not happening. You need some more help. Use the Violet Ray of Transformation. Your intent is to transmute your past problem into Light, to *release* it from your mind and transform it into a higher vibration. So the problem no longer has any power over you and no longer fills you with remorse or anger. There are no what if's or buts. You are now able to look on it as an experience to learn from without any negative emotion. Through this process you can release and transform. The Rays are great healing tools. If you're not sure which ray to use, simply close your eyes and ask. A colour will be shown to you by your own higher self which is always exactly what you need for your highest good at that moment.

That's the job of your higher self. To lead and guide you through this life time of experience. The trick is to watch and listen to all those inner feelings and synchronicities. Begin to pay attention to these, quietly, before your conscious mind steps in and creates doubt. Remember when you meet someone, and you know in a split second whether you like that person or not. That's you're your higher self at work trying to tell you through your feelings. It's your own intuition. You see the soul holds a memory, so it pays to listen carefully.

A Higher Consciousness

Now I want to talk about meditation and just how important it is. I have given you meditations on the Cosmic Rays in a very simply format. They were a mini meditation, an introduction. The Cosmic Rays allowed you to expand your own Light body, to experience a different reality and develop your higher consciousness further. The simplistic way Master Kuthumi gave you the Rays formed a good foundation for you. The meditations were brief yet gave you what you needed, whichever ray you chose.

There is no time limit to any meditation. It is more about the connection and of course your own intention with that particular meditation. We are all made up of dual energies—yin and yang. Our intent directs which side our energies we will flow to—the positive or negative. Master Kuthumi called 2009 a Master Year. It was to be a year of testing for many. Testing of your faith, your strengths, your life focus. At the same time you were being asked to align with your soul energies. 2009 was the preparation toward 2012. The steps we have taken you through so far attest to this.

You have been given many cosmic tools to help you in the process of transformation. That's what this book is about. Overcoming your wounds, finding your inner strengths, your truths and creating a new way forward in your life, stronger and 'Lighter' than before.

Photon Belt Energy

The energies now are interesting. Very similar to the days of Atlantis. We have entered into the Photon Belt energy in the Universe. At the time of writing Earth is smack bang in the centre of what is being called the Galactic equator. This is a band of moving energy in the Universe containing very high vibrational particles which are already comfortably existing in the Earth's atmosphere. This energy has helped mankind to raise his vibrational level considerably.

Prior to this we had the great cosmic shift in the year 2000 which was in preparation for the Photon Belt energy shifts. We are still moving through this high frequency Photon Belt of energy. It has begun the process of altering mankind's DNA. This is to assist us in the opening of our Pineal Gland. Some call this the Master Gland in your body because it connects directly to the Light energies. The powerful Cosmic Rays come under this as well. It is the gateway of As Above, So Below. Yet this gland is only the size of a pea. Isn't that amazing? It contains the power, and the consciousness to govern the frequency of Light particles you will absorb into your bodies, and also which dimensional level you can connect to at any one time.

There have been many great cosmic shifts since. More higher energetic particles arrived in another event on the 9th day of the 9th month 2009. This shift encouraged all of us to raise our level of thought and action to those of love. It is so interesting if you look you can see how lovingly mankind is being guided to higher levels of consciousness by a greater power I prefer to call God.

These shifts continued through to 2012. That long awaited dated of 21th December 2012. Up until that date man was experiencing a new birthing, and there was a lot of personal pain. Some would say there still is. The more inner work you have achieved the more prepared you will be.

Cosmic Laws

I think of these as Cosmic Laws really because they operate at a much higher level than our earthly laws. They resemble God's way. They are truth and cannot be altered. They have been taught in the great Mystery schools throughout our history. It makes sense since we are all raising our vibration; it is now timely to receive these higher guide lines contained in the Cosmic Laws. We begin with the Law of Energy.

The Law of Energy

This involves foremost your thoughts. Words follow your thoughts. Words contain energy also. Actions follow your words. Again, energy is involved. But which energy do you choose to use? This decision contains the balance between ascension and remaining stagnant. Read on for what is so gloriously illustrated in the importance of the correct use of free will. What great lessons we all have the opportunity of learning. The learning is in your decision, then your chosen experience from that decision.

Many years ago Master Kuthumi gave to his young scribe Krishnamurti the four main points for living in a correct and high vibrational way. Those four points were titled—
Discrimination
Desirelessness
Good Conduct
Love.
He also spoke of the intense desire to free himself from all worldly limitations, thereby receiving and attaining, union with God.

So clearly it is only by filling yourself with Divine Love and operating from a place of that Divine Love you can experience absolute freedom. So you see why we say to you so many times that intent is all. Ensure you have correct intent in every undertaking.

**Your intent programmes
your attitude**

So the energy flows further out to the action, and further, to the Ethers. You may feel one action is unimportant, one word won't matter. I got angry—so what? So what indeed. Do you remember that word we gave you? You know the one—*Delete.* Please use it in those angry moments. At the very least it can dissipate some of that dark energy you directed into the Ethers of our planet. You see—The Law of Energy. God requires you operate from a place of peace, a place of love, with a correct attitude in all your undertakings.

Let's just think for a moment here. All those times you got on the phone and gossiped, the times you met a friend for coffee and ended up gossiping about someone else. So why do you do it? Why do some really enjoy it? It's gone on for years hasn't it? You saw your mother, or your grand mother having a chat over the fence. Chances where, some level of gossip was involved.

We know it takes 21 days to change a habit. Yet this can be truly accomplished if you choose to change. Just think, you would not only stop all that negative energy building up around our planet, your words would stop shredding the aura of the poor person you were literally pulling to bits!

Negative energy builds quickly. You gossip for ten minutes which leaves a little pile of dark energy. The person you are gossiping with also leaves a little pile of negative energy. Add it to your pile. Let's say you do this on average four times a day. Add twenty eight piles of dark energy, PLUS the other person in the conversation, that's fifty six piles of DARK energy! Then multiply that by a few billion people! My, my. Try adding up a year. Do you see? This is what happens with just ten minutes of gossip. I don't know about you but I can really see why we are asked to speak with love. Makes you think doesn't it?

Like Attracts Like

This is another sub law tied to the Law of Energy. Remember the magnetic vibration sent out from your sub conscious mind? Like attracts like. So what energy are you attracting to you? Again you can see Divine wisdom at work. There are no idle thoughts. God in His wisdom is showering our planet with beautiful Light enhancing particles. These particles work with your higher self to open you further and to assist you in creating heaven on Earth. If you acknowledge this Divine energy and live with it 24/7, what could you create? Can you imagine? I can. We would all join as one in peace, and begin creating what we want—a new Earth.

Heaven on Earth. All of mankind, now and during the next thirty years do have the power and now the knowledge to bring this into our reality, into being. Like attracts like. This is the one law you need to remember in all things. No more regrets. No more wishing you had done something differently. Only you control your thoughts. There is no need to stay in the lower dimensions any longer. Man has been working his way forward for centuries. We met the crossroads in the year 2000. Heaven's answer was to send a huge energy shift to begin to 'let your love flow' as the song says. Now thirteen years later you are seeing more Light on the planet than ever. Remember this when you experience little pot holes on your road of life. Everyone has Light available to them now. Look to your Balloon Rays. Each one a powerful energy to assist you in your hour of need.

Meet the Masters of Each Ray

*1ˢᵗ **Ray*** is mid blue and usually associated with Master El Moyra, Master El Moyra stands for protection, faith and Will to enrich your relationship with God on this first ray. *Your* Higher Will made action through the full understanding of His Higher Will.

*2ⁿᵈ **Ray*** of Illumination, understanding and wisdom used to be the ray of Master Kuthumi. It is the Yellow Ray and Master Kuthumi often still uses his yellow cloak for many of his faithful students. However Lord Lanto has now taken on the role of the second ray, and is also training many to embrace the Christ Conscious energy.

*3ʳᵈ **Ray*** used in the pink balloon is Ray of Love, also compassion and creativity. This is the ray of Master Paul the Venetian who presides over all artistic souls, in particular those blessed with the gift of music. He encourages one to see beauty in all things and to fulfil their Divine plan.

*4ᵗʰ **Ray*** is the White Ray of purity, harmony and the disciple energy which is watched over by Master Serapis Bay. He assists those using self discipline to prepare and work with the Holy Spirit energy. He also encourages one to work with all of nature.

*5ᵗʰ **Ray*** is the Emerald Green Ray for healing, abundance and truth and is overseen by Master Hilarian. Having a wonderful sense of humour, this Master also leads those out of dark places on their life path, encouraging them to come to the Light. He also prepares one to acknowledge their soul gift of healing, and encourages the opening of the third eye. The Emerald Green Ray is also the Ray of Abundance. The challenge this brings is to achieve balance in its power.

6th Ray introduces Lady Nada. This is the Purple and Gold Ray of peace, service and brother/sisterhood. Lady Nada holds the energy of Divine love for all. The more you learn to love yourself, the more her energy will flow through you if you invite her presence.

7th Ray is Saint Germaine's Violet Ray. His ray holds the great power of transformation into Light, using the energies of the Universal mind. Faith is required in the use of the Violet Flame energy.

We have another balloon colour for you to use as well. The red balloon is associated with strength and power. It can be used for this if you desire. But it can also assist you in developing Divine Will.

All of the Ascended Masters of the Great White Brotherhood, now also known as the Council Of Light, have lived on Earth. They are able to understand the temptations and the heavy energy on Earth, (though now beginning to lift). They know what is needed to gain the strength to overcome and to ascend to the Divine kingdom. This is why they stay close to the Earth realm, to help mankind especially at this great time on Earth.

These Masters help us to learn and understand that we must begin to change our conscious thoughts. This does require discipline, yes. But even this doesn't need to be difficult. Not if you go moment by moment, day by day.

Just one day at a time.

Simply focus on this. Use your new tools of enlightenment in this book! By engulfing yourself in any of the Ray energies, you will shift your focus to one of a higher vibration. It's not that difficult, it merely requires you to remember. When your conscious mind endeavours to remember your soul also opens. It brings higher energies to the surface of your being. Like attracts like energy.

Forgiveness Equals all You Desire

Although we have briefly discussed this, it is such an important key to man's entire future so I will mention it here among the energies of the Masters. What better place? It is only through forgiveness that we attain all we desire—inner peace, joy, warmth of heart. If you continue to hold threads of darkness—threads of anger, jealousy or resentment—how can you hope to transcend to the Light? The darkness must be transmuted through forgiveness first. You can use your cosmic tools here to help you get to the point of forgiveness, but you must forgive from your heart. In other words *mean it*. A half attempt will not do, no. In the forgiveness you let go. You may not forget, but you let go. Did you ever think you could be so free? Many have shared their feelings of joy and freedom after great acts of forgiveness. They just let go and decided not to carry the burden any longer. In doing so they claimed victory.

The Master of Forgiveness

This was of course, Jesus. What a beautiful Light he is. He taught many how to forgive and always encouraged forgiveness. The ego uses your emotional and mental bodies. Yet Master Kuthumi has reminded you many times that recognition is 80%. So it is for you to be diligent in recognizing when the ego self is seeking to take control of you through your thoughts and emotions. Recognize it. Put up your STOP sign. Realign to the Light and move forward. This is the remaining 20%. In this way you can learn to control your ego self which is part of you. Part of your duality, part of your learning. Just as you practice forgiveness as the key to ascension, you also practice control over your ego self through self discipline. Something to remember and practice—

> **In that moment of recognition, ask yourself—do I choose Light, or darkness?**

That moment is your crossroad and it's very powerful. There is another aspect to this, one that may surprise you. Some people stay very smug while holding on very tightly to their resentment and anger of another. They hold it as though they are holding a treasure chest, guarding it while feeding it with more negative emotion as they relive the memory over and over. They somehow feel a power in this. Some say," I won't forget what you did, I'll remember." And they do—frequently! The problem is the negative emotions attached to that memory. This is what holds them down and back.

If only they could realize that they are making the other person involved a winner all over again. That other person is still managing to hold power over them. Still managing to keep them down in negativity. All the while, that negative energy is building deep within. So I ask you again, who is the victor?

Have you had an 80% moment? Have you suddenly realized this is you and you don't want it to be you? Then use the other 20%. Forgive and move on with your life. Take your power back! This doesn't mean you approve of the other person's actions, or that you won't think of it again. What it does mean is that you have taken control of it. The situation or person no longer has any power over you. You have taken control of this issue in your emotional body. So next time you think of it, you're not angry, bitter or hurt. You just remember and keep moving forward. You will feel more powerful and happier too. By now you must know you are never truly alone. There's a whole world out there on the next dimension and the next, and the next.

The Law of Integrity

There have been many unseen Light workers throughout history. One was Abraham Lincoln. He said this:

> **"I am not bound to win, but I am bound to be true. I am not bound to succeed, but I am bound to live up to what Light I have."**

What profound words. These very words penetrate your soul and stir you to remember personal integrity. You see it's not about winning or losing, it's how you ran the race that matters. Personal integrity is born of your own heart. It's how you behave when you think no one is watching. Of course God is, though many forget this.

It's also about following your higher wisdom. Listening, watching and following through with correct action. One that's true to who you are, and true to God. To simply be yourself—your heart self. If you break a Universal Law, then you learn through that action. There can be no escape from the learning. It will be presented, if not in this lifetime, then the next. This is how we learn and our soul grows through experience and chosen action.

To live in integrity you need to know yourself. The good, the bad and the ugly as it were. All of you and in that knowing comes an acceptance—a higher acceptance. One that doesn't judge you, nor criticize you when you fall down. Your higher self simply accepts, makes the necessary adjustments, and moves on in acceptance. It's your ego self that can't truly accept you and seeks to pull you down through doubt and sadness. Yet there is a lesson here. A valuable one. You must overcome your ego, understand and control it, in order to fully accept yourself as you are in your totality. To say to the world—this is me as I am! Can you do that? Can you live your own truth, your own integrity? In this way you Light the way for others. Then—you will receive even more Light yourself!

Chapter Fifteen

Reaching New Heights

Master Kuthumi has told me to cover meditation to make sure you fully understand what it is and how to do it. I think most will know that being in a meditation will take you to a higher level if done correctly. Some people I have met however think that meditation is simply closing your eyes and having a conversation in your mind, mainly with yourself. This is NOT meditation. It is conscious mind talk to yourself.

A Guide to Meditating

So how do you get to a higher dimension and learn how to connect to your angels and guides? Firstly realize that your guides are not going to hit you over the head and shout at you just so you know they're there! They work on a subtle energetic level. But I'm getting ahead of myself. You need to prepare your space if you are intending to meditate inside. Of course if you are outside you don't really need any preparation because you use the trees and the grass. Just perhaps somewhere quiet away from traffic and people.

So back to inside the home. Let's say you've decided on what will be your own quiet meditative area. You will need a comfortable chair that fully supports your body. You may want a small table beside you for a candle, water or a recording device. Many find a darkened room is better so you may need to close the curtains. It's also nice to have some soft music playing. It's a matter of choosing what you like and which will help you feel relaxed. Now your space is set, let's go to the next step.

It helps a great deal to take the phone off the hook while you are meditating. You don't want to be disturbed. It's essential you learn to completely relax your physical body as you begin. This can be achieved in sections. For example, I always begin at the feet and legs. Next the tummy muscles and torso. Then the hands and arms. Don't forget those large shoulder muscles and the throat area. Remember your face muscles and finally the mind. Take your time for this relaxation process. It will get faster and easier with practice.

Still Your Mind with Master Kuthumi

The mind is often the most difficult, especially for those who have a 'busy mind.' Many say they can't stop the chatter of their minds. Well you can, but it does require self discipline and as I said, practice.

Master Kuthumi gave a wonderful solution for this actually. He suggested if you have difficulty overcoming a chattering mind as you begin, focus on a small ball of white Light about ten inches above your head. Visualize it and focus on that white ball. Then if busy thoughts again enter your mind, send them away and bring your attention back to that white ball of Light. At first you may find your self refocusing on the Light frequently. Don't worry. You are retraining your mind to be still when you want it to be. It's very important to keep going and keep refocusing on that ball of Light.

You will find after a short time that you need to refocus less and less. So be kind to yourself. This is such an important step and a great personal accomplishment. You <u>will</u> find one day as you prepare and relax your body, that mind chatter has gone.

On to the next step.

You need to do the three breath exercise, again given by Master Kuthumi. This exercise is important on an energetic level because it realigns and shifts your subtle bodies and opens the Pineal gland. We have touched on this wonderful little Master Gland previously. The three breath exercise creates a 'flip' of this gland as it opens to allow the Light particles of energy to enter your body. This gland is the gateway to the higher realms and Spirit. The three breath exercise is simple and effective, but you do need to remember one simple rule. Always <u>completely</u> fill your lungs with air on the inward breath. So let's run through it.

Relax the body and sit quietly.

Breathe in deeply through the nose, completely filling your lungs with air until you feel they'll burst.

Now <u>slowly</u> release the air through your mouth.

Repeat

Fill your lungs completely once more, but on the third outward breath, release all the events and energies of the day and all events you're holding on to. Just imagine them all falling away from you on that outward breath. Let it all fall away.

Breathe gently, peacefully. You should feel a subtle release and a shift in your energy field.

All tensions, worries, concerns should be gone in this moment as you leave your earthly emotions and problems behind.

This is another crucial step in meditation. You will not succeed in your meditation if you are unable to release your worries etc. One of the reasons may be because your ego self will attempt to step right in and 'chatter' about a concern or something that happened that day to try to bring you back to the conscious mind and physical reality. You see when you meditate the ego self is left behind. But to distract you it will attempt to pull you back to problems. Be aware of this.

Remember you are doing the most important thing you could do— get in touch with your higher self and your spirit guides. You are in charge now. It's helpful to remember Master Kuthumi's ball of white Light to focus on.

The next step is to imagine yourself rising to that ball of white Light, reaching it, and entering that white Light energy. Feeling it all around you. You'll feel more peaceful than you've ever felt before. Now just rest in that energy. Get used to it, how it feels—that wonderful peace.

Some of you will achieve this step faster than others. It doesn't matter. Persevere.

To help you rise higher in the dimensions, Master Kuthumi suggests visualizing a golden 'rope' for you to climb up. From the top of your head to the ball of Light, visualize yourself climbing up that golden rope. Focus. These are aspects of yourself. Once you reach the ball of Light, rest. You have now reached a meditative state. No monkey mind, just a very peaceful state. You will also feel quite weightless. You simply just are. You may be slightly aware of the physical but it will hold no importance. It will feel a long way away from you, almost in the distance. What you feel is similar to the first stages of waking from a dream, or a deep state of day dreaming. Totally relaxed and on another dimension.

When you achieve this state, anything is possible. You realize that, yes, there is another world many cannot see, but they can *feel* it.

It's all energy!

Great healing is available on this level. As I've said everything is energy, and that energy filters through to your mental, emotional and physical bodies. It seeps down into every cell healing and cleansing on the way, depositing a feeling of peace, of floating on air. So you see meditation has many benefits.

It's worthwhile to seek out a local meditation group in your area. I have taught many groups during my many years on this path. It is such a joy to see a person develop, to witness the light in their eyes when they 'get' it. The excitement. It's just wonderful. In a group you will often become friends with many there. As you meditate together, usually in a circle, all of the energies join and merge. As time goes by your conscious mind gets used to all the others energies in the group. You feel more at home as this occurs.

Of course you can share after the meditation as well. This is very valuable information as you listen to what others have experienced in the meditation. Often experiences will be different. But perhaps you are a bit reluctant to speak of your experience and then suddenly someone else in the group speaks of something similar. Wow. You're not weird after all. This is a great way to learn meditation and to make some great new friends as well. So do consider looking for a group. One last word however. Do be sure you are comfortable with your teacher—her way of doing the meditation, and her energy. Because if you're not, you will never relax in her group and sadly, will never progress forward. It is vital you feel comfortable.

Most meditation groups will cover metaphysical development as well. This is great as it is an opportunity to gain a higher understanding of spirit and the dimensions. Once you understand how everything works in the higher realms it makes everything so easy. It really does.

The Energy of Earth—the Lay Lines

In the days of Atlantis, there was an electromagnetic grid deep in the Earth. Crystals were used in transmitting energy from the grid. The people of Atlantis were highly evolved beings. The grid formed a connection between Heaven and Earth through the energy of the grid and spirit. Today we have Lay Lines on Earth. Just as the full electromagnetic grids worked on waves of energy which was picked up by the brain, the Lay Lines also send out energetic waves as well, although of course, not as powerful—yet!

Vortexes occur where two positive Lay Lines meet. Often springs of pure water can be found nearby as well. Water diviners often connect to these Lay Lines to find water. The Lay Lines contain high levels of energy. The Pineal gland contains fluids, mainly water. You see how all is connected through the electromagnetic energy grids and Lay Lines. I believe animals connect to these energies too. It's been well documented how animals send out warnings in their behaviour prior to weather disasters. They pick up the energy waves transmitted through the Earth and air.

There are of course waves of energy in our atmosphere. I have referred to this often, as has Master Kuthumi. The crystals placed in the Earth and ourselves—even our Pineal gland contains minuet crystals—connect to these energetic waves creating a web of energy which is infused with the energy of the Divine.

As Above, So Below

We know that crystals—particularly the Quartz family—radiate electromagnetic energies. Humans also radiate an electromagnetic energy field. The high priests of Atlantis, who were women, worked in the magnificent large crystal chambers. They could sustain the vast energy and the heat radiated from that energy. Today man struggles to stay in a similar crystal chamber for any length of time. It's just too hot. It's interesting that the higher the energy the more heat humans feel in the physical body.

But the people of Atlantis were healed of all negative energy including negative thoughts in the great crystal chambers. The intensity needed by each individual determined how long one would stay in a particular chamber. The energies of the crystal also reflected where one did their 'time.' Today, we would relate to this time as prison time. However in Atlantis this method of healing one's negative behaviour was very successful. Crime was almost non-existent. Some of the crystal chambers were could be 40 feet high and filled with multiple columns of clear quartz, smoky quartz, amethyst or rose quartz. I believe other crystals were added to these too depending on the healing needs of the patient.

The priests worked on the Etheric body, the mental and emotional bodies to clear any impure thoughts which had related to the negative behaviour. They believed such thoughts lead to improper behaviour and crime. How true! Of course the energy fields of the priests were very high. They may have also used hands on healing as well for their patients, transmitting energy to particular spots in the auric field. The energy from these crystal caverns also radiated out along the Lay Lines of Earth. This kept the Lay Lines strong and energized.

So with this magnificent crystal grid so energized, it kept Earth and mankind in a high vibrational field of Light. Peace reigned supreme—for quite a time. But sadly as history tells us Atlantis fell and much was lost.

In the last few years a new crystal grid has been formed. Light beings and planetary shifts have assisted in this process. As man understands more about energy, gateways have been discovered around the planet once more. A higher consciousness has been reached again, though there is still a higher level to attain. Conditions are once again ready to support a raised consciousness using telepathic communication and healing energies.

Many Light workers are connecting to this grid. We can connect to others around the planet, send healing and messages to others not in our presence. But many humans are still unaware.

The energy cannot be misused

Only those of a sufficiently high vibration can gain access to the grid's energies.

Each time you experience another energy shift in the planet the grid is fired and more higher energy is released around our planet. This energy encourages us to release our outdated behaviours and issues. Not to keep hoarding them away on our emotional body.

Recently you hear many people complaining there is so much anger and frustration everywhere, things seem to be going wrong in their lives. Mankind is being asked to release all that anger and frustration, to adjust their lives and live simply and peacefully. To let go of the rush and bustle of dancing to others demands. They may have less material possessions, but they will be far happier and a lot more relaxed with their integrity intact.

It's sad that so many make excuses why they can't create this scenario for themselves and their families. They don't seem to understand that they create what they will experience each day, each month, each year. So I have to ask, "How much do you want peace in your life?" You cannot have this existence with no effort on your part. The reality is quite different. You have to create it. You have to choose. The Universe has made a new grid. Now it's up to mankind.

The Law of Surrender

Can we surrender? Are we willing? What is Divine Will? Am I safe?

Well of course you know you are safe when you are experiencing Divine Grace, you can't be safer than that. Mankind has been somewhat brainwashed with seeds of untruths which bound man to lives of struggle and poverty. The reason for this was power, money and control. But this is the past. Understand this—the past.

When we decide to surrender in Light, in love, we surrender to the higher Will of God. We let go of the parts of our old selves which no longer serve us. It is as always our choice to do so. No one is ever forced. However once you begin to experience the freedom of higher understanding, the complete inner peace, then you simply don't want the old 'rat race' anymore. The worry, the tiredness, the negative energies—no more! So you let go. You decide to change your life. It's interesting some are now calling this their 'water shed moments.'

You begin to understand new truths, new ideas, those which sit well in your heart. You think about your own values and in doing all this you begin to create a new reality, a new life for yourself. A new adventure. Because you are coming form your heart you automatically embrace a higher will. You transform your feelings, your perspective of life and the varied situations that happen every day. There may still be some challenges to overcome. But it's your perception that has changed when you surrender to a higher will—the Divine presence. This also works in looking at what you have and what you receive. Many spend so much time and energy fretting and worrying over so much during their day. They worry about what they have and haven't done and what others say or didn't say. They see an injustice and want to fight for truth. They can fight for truth, but it will be so much more effective from a higher will perspective. Ask yourself when faced with one of those trying moments or someone's anger, "What would my Divine will do?"

Your higher self, who is directly linked to your soul, will answer through a feeling, a word, a knowing. Your higher self desires a positive change, a positive outcome, in peace. It isn't wise to waste your energy on matters which you have no control over. That is wasted energy.

When you surrender to a higher will you don't lose your power—you gain it! You become more powerful, free and full of Light. This is a higher power, not a lower ego fed power, so you tend not to worry over the small details so much. You look instead to the bigger picture.

The old way was to push ahead at any cost. To be first at any cost. Some cheated, obscured the facts, anything to win and be acknowledged for that win. But hang on a minute. Do you recognize all this old behaviour comes from the ego? If you can relate to this then STOP, right now. Take a deep breath. Sit quietly and take a good look at your life, then ask, "Do I want this as my reality? Is this how I want to be?" Ask. If your answer is no then begin now to create a new reality from a higher perspective. Change your perception.

> **Perception is projection.**

Anyone can change, anytime—if they choose to. You don't have to stay stuck anywhere, in any situation or behavioural pattern. You choose, you decide. Isn't that great? And you know, as you begin to surrender, as you begin looking at all your situations from a higher place, your focus totally changes. You may even find your self asking, "Why did I put so much energy into that old situation, it's not even important." You've changed your perception for the better.

Man is not perfect. We're human to. Everyone makes mistakes sometimes. So what! The world doesn't stop because you fell down, or made a mistake. Simply recognize it—80%—adjust your perception, and move forward—20%. After a while you will not only have a new perception permanently, you will have developed a new way of looking at life, a new way of overcoming those annoying obstacles that pop up. You're solutions are now coming from your higher self. Things look different from up there. You feel a lot calmer too and you're body will thank you. The stress is all but gone. So isn't it worth a try? To align with your higher self and experience Divine Will.

Man really needs to come back to balance in his life. The thing is it isn't that hard! As the song says, "It's been a long and winding journey, picking up the pieces, bringing joy back into your life." This is where man is today. The wise ones are on Earth to guide you and to show the way forward. As you develop and understand higher knowledge you move out of karmic debt. You release using higher wisdom and unconditional love.

In the new reality you neither incur karma or create it. In days gone by this would have been scorned at as silly illusions, dreams, fantasy. But you know it isn't. In days gone by they didn't have access to the higher knowledge we do today. We are living in magnificent times. Every soul on the planet has incarnated to share in the experience of a raised vibration, a raised energy around Earth and a higher consciousness is being born.

I Am The Light Of The World

Today there are many people who are able to communicate with Jesus, Buddha, God. Some choose not to believe this is possible and so they keep themselves separated from the Light. Why? Perhaps it's because deep down they don't believe they're good enough. Or is it because they truly believe they are mortal and spirit is immortal? So how can they communicate? Is it another's truth, a truth passed down from generation to generation that they choose to be theirs also? Probably many reasons, yet there is so much evidence available today of life after death. Even scientists are catching up with energy, emotions, the Universe and a Divine order.

When a soul steps onto the path of enlightenment, they must also accept Oneness. There are many lessons and experiences on the way. Some call this polishing your gold—or is it your Diamond Light? Your higher heart contains that spark of God Light we all carry within us. That spark that makes all of us the Light of the world when you choose to develop your higher self, to surrender to Divine Will, Divine Light.

These are the steps our ancient wise ones walked. They learned to ascend but stayed in the Etheric to help others and to light the way for us to follow. The Ascended Masters are very active today giving us hope, guidance and love, asking us all to be a Light of the world now when it is needed most.

Chapter Sixteen

Energy Vortexes in the Body

We have spoken a lot about energy and Light, which is of course the highest vibrational energy we know at present. Master Kuthumi will tell you there is another even higher God. He spoke of this last year in his teachings on his web site. His purpose is to lead us ever higher, toward a Universal God, so high, so bright, we can scarcely imagine. Yet this does exist.

But before we go totally above the clouds I want to talk about your own energy vortexes. Many call these chakras which as you know is an old Sanskrit word. I call them vortexes because of their shape like a long horn, or cornucopia, which resides in your Etheric body. The energy flows through your outer energy field called the Aura, through to the vortex centres, where the energy then filters through to the physical body. Your energy field continually moves and flows according to your emotional, mental and physical wellbeing, as well as your spiritual state and what you pick up from the immediate environment. All these factors affect your energy levels a great deal.

The stem of a vortex has a valve which can close off. These valves can be damaged by alcohol and drug use. The valve may even get stuck in the open phase which allows unwanted energies to flow through to your other bodies—the emotional, mental and physical. This scenario can be healed by an experienced healer which is encouraging, but it may take three or four sessions to repair a vortex centre.

There is a central column which is referred to as the Hara line in Reiki healing. I see this as a golden rod which lies against the spine in the Etheric. It's important to keep this rod clear, flowing and energized as each vortex is connected to this rod of intense energy. Remember also that each of the six lower vortexes are fed from the Hara Line, meeting in the centre and expanding out to your front and your back, looking like cones, (vortexes.)

When a baby is born the end of the vortex is closed. Each vortex opens separately as the child grows in age. When closed the end reminds me of the large bud of a flower, tight and closed. Let's look at these essential energy centres in detail.

The Base

The Base or Root vortex (chakra) will open from birth to around three years of age. I associate this vortex with setting boundaries and self preservation. Most will usually dwell within their own boundaries preferring the safe and correct road. Most don't like it when others encroach on these boundaries. Some children in loving, secure homes will develop this vortex sooner than another child in a less loving home.

As the child learns to crawl and walk, new boundaries must be learnt. These are the first steps of independence. Parents who are too strict can cause a child to be quite rebellious. The Base vortex is the first in the basic six vortexes. The colour is red. This is a heavier vibration so it suits this vortex quite well. If you are using the colour red for healing, use one of the softer red hues, a mauve or purple hue. You could even wear one of these colours for your under wear, or just visualize a red hue. Since this is an earthy vibration it is very connected to the physical body. This vortex is associated with skin, bones and muscles. Self esteem is reflected through this vortex as well. Since it is so aligned to your birth, you may like to meditate on the effect your birth had on your parents and family. Ask why you chose them to be your parents and what you need to learn from them? If you are aware your higher self will provide the answers.

The Sacral

The Sacral Vortex, which is just below your belly button, is associated with creativity, sexuality, and security. The development age is around three to seven years of age. This is an important vortex as around five or six most children go to school. They experience separation for longer periods of time from the mother. This can mean a big emotional security issue for a child. This vortex can link to the throat vortex of expression. So if these vortexes do become blocked, your life may seem to be quite unfulfilled and feelings of security while hidden, may be a big issue.

Sibling survival and rivalry play out in the home creating fear instead of joy. Interestingly the colour of this vortex is orange, which is the colour of vitality and creativity. If you can't relate to this colour then your sacral vortex may need clearing. Humans need to feel free, to feel creative, and to enjoy life. Life was not meant to be a big struggle; it was to be experienced as happiness and joy. This vortex also associates with your own inner child. Look back and see how your childhood was from the age of three to seven. Do you need to heal your inner child or let it out to play, to be loved, to be happy? This can be done in meditation. I usually work with Mother Mary for this work. You will know if you need inner child work. Again, your higher self will guide you.

The Solar Plexus

The Solar Plexus vortex lies just below your sternum. This is often called the mid way vortex or chakra. It's where many store all the old, hurtful, emotional baggage. They don't really want to look at it, or know about all that stuff, so all those experiences they can't face are stuffed down to this vortex. That's where most of it ends up, where it's all held. Not surprisingly, this vortex is associated with the digestive system. Also your eyesight and psychic abilities. If this vortex is blocked your psychic abilities will be limited. You may feel you can't go up to the higher dimensions at all.

Children develop very quickly. A child of twelve is seeking new independence and lots of answers. Puberty has begun. It's a huge learning period. It may be here that a child first learns to hide those hurts and issues. Not to face them, but to bury them deep within. The energy of these issues will end up in this vortex.

Your higher self knows when you are harbouring hurts, anger and issues here, so it tries to bring people and situations around you, to bring some of those hurts or issues to the surface to be dealt with, and then released. You see your higher self knows if it isn't dealt with, then the withheld emotion around the event will create an emotional block which will require much deeper work to shift and transmute. Your higher self *always* looks to your highest good.

Blocks and old issues, withheld hurts and anger will always will prevent you from gaining ascension. You will progress on your spiritual path so far and then you seemingly become stuck. You can't progress any further. Some people think that is where they're just supposed to be. They accept that's it. Usually that isn't the case. One way you can find out is to ask. Before you go to sleep ask to be shown anything that you still need to deal with. You may also ask before you enter into a meditative state. Ask to be shown.

Often you get a sample, a small window of the incident, or see a face, or you may hear words you thought you had long forgotten. Remember this is buried deep within so it might be a good idea to enlist some help from a thought field therapist, soul healer or similar Light worker. Chances are you've buried this one very deeply. You may think it's too difficult to look at but it must be released sooner or later. Either in this life time or the next.

The benefits are of course that you can clear and heal the issue. You can also raise your vibration even higher once that heavy hidden emotion is removed. You'll feel so much happier and lighter in yourself. So it really is worthwhile doing.

The colour of this Solar Plexus vortex is yellow. It is here where the ego begins to be felt—think of a young teenager! Your life may feel stuck if this vortex is blocked. Feed it soft yellow colours. You can do this during your meditations by simply visualizing yellow, or wear the colour on your body where your physical eyes can actually see the colour.

The crystal Rose Quartz can be of great assistance to this vortex. The soft pink ray softening and healing stress held here. This may also help teenagers stretching their wings while trying to find their own identity.

The Heart

The Heart Vortex is attached to feelings of love, compassion, tenderness and also detachment. Do you remember your first love? The imagination swelled as they declared their devotion and love for another. A 'crush' is felt so passionately with the intensity of a first love. The young teenager is exploring the emotions of love for another outside of their family circle. New boundaries are being learnt. A rejection may be carried for many years, or shrugged off depending on how much love the child has received in their upbringing. These first experiences form the relationship behavioural patterns you often will carry for life. Teenage years are a very tender and impressionable time and need gentle support from parents if possible.

Many now portray the colour of this vortex as green, though not so long ago it was portrayed as pink. Green is more of an intense healing colour, so perhaps this is one of the reasons why it was changed. We seem to need really intense healing as mankind transits into a new era based on love. So I guess the colour green is really needed for us to heal hurts and pain. You can always use pink later as it is a softer energy. No one can deny they need love to function properly in a balanced manner. Babies who are held and loved thrive in their development. Those who are not shown such love develop much slower.

Feeling loved is vital to your well being. When one doesn't feel love at all they merely exist. The crystal rose or watermelon Tourmaline will help a heart that is blocked emotionally, or is even shut off due to trauma or loss.

Some years ago, Master Kuthumi channelled to me The Emerald Heart meditation, as I have mentioned, for both mankind and the planet. It's now available as a download on his website www.kuthumischool.com During this meditation; it would be a good time to reflect on how you function in the world and how you see others.

The Throat

The Throat Vortex is next. Everyone knows where this vortex is located I think—the throat. The colour is mid to deep blue. The Heart Vortex is thought of as the gateway, flowing down to the Base Vortex, and up to the Crown Vortex. The Throat Vortex merges with all, being the vortex of expression. Depending on your vibration you will either seek a higher expression, or a lower 'me' expression.

The Throat Vortex encompasses both upper and lower—yin and yang—energies.

Between the ages of fifteen to twenty one you begin to develop your firm opinions and core truths. You begin to think who you will <u>choose</u> to relate to in your life. Prior to this you may have given very little thought to whether you really like others in your group circle. This may sound strange but teenagers often simply like to be included. They will put up with and tolerate a lot just to feel included.

As they reach eighteen to nineteen years of age they are faced with taking charge of their lives a lot more. Taking responsibility. The first is usually around the issue of daily work. There are many issues involved—your workmates, your labour verses money you're paid, balancing your work and play times. Big responsibilities. Taking care of yourself. Setting new boundaries—again!

How do you feel about it all? How will you communicate to a different set of people now—workmates, a boss, and another authority figure?

> **Communication is the cornerstone of your life.**

As babies you cry for food, attention and to be touched, loved. To be picked up, to feel that communication with another through touch. This is the first expression of communication you experience. When you speak you learn another form of communication. Then you learn to assess and communicate with new authority figures outside of home and family—school teachers. Later in life you struggle to express your feelings of love for another—the first 'crush.' Then the need to communicate on a different level again as you enter the work force. Another authority figure, but this one has power over your livelihood.

These people may or may not be of your choice yet you must find middle ground if you are to survive. If you are unable to find a place of middle ground then you need to learn the art of tolerance and detachment. And so it goes on for the rest of your life. Friends will come and go. Some will stay and become very treasured and important in your life—a rare jewel, a life long friend.

The gospel of John: In the beginning was the word, and the word was with God. So communication has always been our main form of interacting with another. At a higher level we can look at the collective consciousness. We are connected through the Divine— the Christ Consciousness. Terminology. Many it seems get quite caught up in terminology. Many various words and expressions have the same meaning, yet use different words, especially in various languages. Why do some insist it is only their words which are correct? They don't really bother to ask or to try to understand what another's words mean. This is the lower form of communication.

The higher form has compassion for all and understands we are part of One, and is prepared to ask and to understand the meaning of another's words if the expression differs from their own. It has long been thought that the age of twenty one represents the 'coming of age.' Where you are seen as an adult in society. Perhaps given where mankind is today in his collective development, we should be looking at a higher level of communication. That of communicating with Spirit, with our higher self, and with God. The following vortexes lead us into the higher vortex levels. These vortexes are used as you develop your higher senses, your spiritual gifts.

The Brow

The first of these is the Brow Vortex. It is associated with insight, spirit and what is known as the Third Eye. Let me explain this as many read about a Third eye but may not completely understand it.

You have your physical eyes which are able to see everything around you in a physical sense. You can see a book to read, the sky, birds and trees etc. With the Third Eye, you are able to see on another dimension of existence. A dimension of energy, vibration, a world of Spirit. It is on the Etheric level. At first you may see colour, Light, shadows, all which exist on another dimension, a higher level of consciousness. This level is usually not seen with the physical eyes, though some people are now able to. These ones can exist between the dimensions, two or more levels at once while still at a conscious level. As above, so below.

When you meditate, you are able to see the next dimension. As you expand your higher consciousness you are able to access other higher dimensions and levels of existence. It may not happen straight away. You must learn to let go of old emotions first. Yes, this has been mentioned repeatedly throughout this book, but perhaps now you begin to more fully understand the importance of letting go. Why it is so essential to your future. It's no wonder we call it a 'journey.' Yet a miraculous one you will agree, where you connect to your Soul, your higher self.

> **Connectedness is a key word
> for the throat vortex.**

Connectedness is where you learn to communicate with ALL of you. Your body, your emotions, your mind, Spirit, Soul, God. Yes, God.

All of us carry a spark, a Diamond Light of God's Essence within us. This is our connection to the Divine, to His word, His infinite love which is pure and cannot be tainted.

The Light energy you connect to when you meditate is part of the Divine Consciousness energy. The Rays we discussed earlier are also part of the same Divine Conscious energy. Let me ask you, "When you meditate deeply and you return feeling such a depth of inner peace, where do you think that energy came from?"

You have touched on the Divine Essence. The deeper the connection in meditation, the longer that feeling of deep inner peace and connectedness will stay with you. This feeling is almost indescribable. But you *feel it!* The feeling can last up to two days or longer at times. Your Soul receives and stores the experience gained from Spirit. It holds the vibration you know as pure Bliss! You experience a timeless existence in this state.

As you work with the Brow Vortex you may begin to meet various Arch Angels, your own Spirit Guides and the various Masters of the higher realms—all messengers of God. They are available to love and guide us, to expand our higher awareness and understanding. Master Kuthumi said in 2001,

> *"Through knowledge comes understanding, and understanding releases fear."*

How true. How very true. This is what the Masters, guides and Arch Angels seek to do, to teach you, to give you a new understanding. When you open to a higher awareness and understanding, your lower existence is seen very differently so you often begin to see people around you quite differently. You see what level they are operating from. If it is a lower level you experience, perhaps for the first time, a disconnection from that person. You don't like what you are seeing in that person. You are seeing them as they are, or more correctly, *where* they are on the levels of consciousness.

They may be operating from pure ego and be materialistic or selfish but you will see it all. I have noticed and spoken to many people who have experienced this as they awakened to the higher realms.

It is also perhaps, the first big spiritual test. For if you judge or condemn them, you take yourself back to the lower vortex levels. Rather, you need to learn to look using your higher understanding and compassion. Remember not so long ago you were there. You now see through 'new' eyes. It's good to remember this as this will help you to look with compassion. To understand that when that person is ready, they too will experience a shift in consciousness just as you did.

Chapter Seventeen

The Higher Energy Vortexes

Now we reach the highest vibrational vortex beyond the six main vortexes. You will note that each vortex focuses on a higher level of vibration. Your consciousness rises also to allow you to connect and work at that higher level.

The Crown

The Crown Vortex is at the top of the head, interestingly where the fontanel area is on a baby's head. This is the vortex that creates the first connection to your Soul—the first connection to higher consciousness. When you connect fully through this vortex to the Light, you surrender. You leave behind your physical body and ego self—some call this the shadow self—all is left behind as you surrender in love to a higher Divine Will.

As you connect to the Light—which enters through this vortex— your Thymus Vortex is opened also and together working in unison connect you to the higher consciousness. You release and surrender in Bliss! Those of you who have experienced this cannot deny the great peace and contentment you feel. This vortex connects directly to the Pineal gland and the Pituitary glands and opens the Third Eye to receive insights and higher guidance. The Crown Vortex connects to the Soul; hence Master Kuthumi's term Soul Light, which he often uses in his teachings and channellings.

Through each lifetime you come to Earth to learn through various experiences, both good and not so good. Yet all is experience— learning through your chosen actions and the choices you make. You also learn to bring balance to your life. You learn to balance your higher and ego selves. Many are now calling the ego self the shadow self. If people understand this term better then what does it matter? It's merely terminology after all.

But you balance all. Your will—you surrender and balance to the Divine will. You balance judgement with compassion. You balance yourself with unconditional love for all. And all the while as you learn these vital lessons, you raise your vibrational level higher and higher. As this occurs these things seem to be quite natural for you to do. You actually <u>want</u> to live this way and to have this balance in your life. Why? Because you are operating from a higher plane of existence. If you look at the areas above where you create a balance and you think, "Oh no, I can't do that," then you are needing to work at raising your vibrational energy level. It's a natural progression for us after all.

Building Your Light Quotient

Do this by raising your Light Quotient. This is the amount of Light you carry within you and within your auric field. Build it up by meditating frequently, sitting in the Light essence, surrounding yourself with Light, breathing it in deeply, holding it within for some time and allowing every cell to be bathed in the Light essence. Do this often and you will find yourself operating from a higher consciousness in your daily life and in your choices. You are now building your Light Quotient you see. No one can take this from you—no one. It is this level of Light you carry with you when you pass over. It is the only thing you take with you from Earth.

You yourself are the only one who can take it away through very determined choices. But even then it only leaves your conscious mind. The more Light you hold then of course you will not want to turn away at all. Why would you? You have found an inner peace, a greater wisdom; your heart has opened in a different way. A way of unconditional love. I haven't yet met a person who would wish to turn their back on this. And so, you complete your karmic journey.

Your Karmic Journey

We have all come to do this. All who are incarnated now on Earth. Even those who cross over at a young age. The way they pass is sometimes karmic. So a great cycle is completed. I remember the many, many ones who have come to me for guidance over the last fourteen years especially. I can tell you the main theme has been relationships. Relationships of all kinds, lovers, husbands, wives, children, friends, business partners, all of it. Problems, so many problems—all around relationship issues.

Many were ending a karmic relationship. Many didn't understand why certain people reacted the way they did. The Universe was giving them a golden opportunity to look deeper, to listen to their Soul. Some did however, and they found the answers they needed at that time. But many didn't and now, fourteen years later, they're finally getting it and some are opening to a new way. Building bridges instead of destroying them. Beginning to understand that they are a small part in a tapestry known as the evolution of mankind.

The Greatest Play of All Time

And so you learn and you understand a new way of communicating on a daily basis. You open to the Light, healing, visions and higher knowledge. This automatically flows out to the people you meet each day. So you communicate in a different way on a conscious level. You begin to see through the greatest play of all time.

You see through the actions of others to see their ego self fighting for control. At that point you attain enlightenment. You understand and release your own selfish self. Not in blind obedience, but in higher understanding and unconditional love. You develop trust and faith. Two words. Simple words, yet man has so much trouble developing these two words. I believe because power and greed have ruled over us. But now thankfully I feel man is beginning to open his eyes and to view a much bigger picture with a greater understanding. The Crown Vortex opens you to these great steps. If you connect to your soul level through this vortex you can begin to see and understand your purpose in this life time.

Soul Memory Blocks

Sometimes in a previous life, you have experienced a situation you still haven't dealt with. You have chosen not to. This has created a 'block' in the soul memory which has overflowed onto your emotional and mental body in this incarnation. So it is held very deeply within you. Yet your Higher Self will continually bring you people and situations to activate that memory, even though it will be painful. Why else would you try to deny its existence?

My husband Michael has been taught by Masters El Moyra and Jesus to work at this level of healing and release. Michael calls it Soul Healing, though few really understand the significance of it. The Masters are always there and the work I can say has been channelled and guided. It is very humbling to see.

Of course the Crown Vortex is a doorway to the higher realms and is the meeting point between the higher realms, your own Etheric body and your conscious mind. It's the door you step through to meditate, to meet with the angelic realm, the Masters and guides. I like to remember the spirit helpers because they do so much on an unseen level.

Quantum Consciousness

You may think all of the higher vortexes are above the Crown Vortex but there is one very important vortex I wish to mention that isn't. It is closely linked to the higher heart and is called the Thymus Vortex.

The Thymus

The colour is Aqua. Interestingly a mix of the Heart and Throat Vortex colours. It's the perfect shade for this vortex I feel. You just need to rest in the energy of this vortex to feel cleared and at peace at a higher level. The Thymus Vortex sits appropriately between the Heart and Throat Vortexes. It is very appropriate because man must learn to communicate with each other in a new way. Some refer to this vortex as the Higher Heart Vortex/ chakra. It is God's filter for us. It's where you can take your daily worries; filter them through this magnificent vortex, then down to your Heart Vortex, and up to your conscious mind to create transmutation of any lower thinking and feelings. To give higher solutions through a higher awareness and a new way of seeing. It brings God's love to **all** situations. It truly is the centre of unconditional love.

But you will need to open and allow yourself to accept. Sadly some cannot accept. Why? Because they do not feel worthy? Master Kuthumi wishes to speak:

> *"I say to them wake up. Shake off your conditioning of childhood. Open yourself consciously to receive. Only you can do this but I*

tell you, this is your <u>only</u> way forward. Gather the courage and take the step. Follow us. Follow our footsteps."

Kuthumi

Through this vortex you will experience a feeling of wholeness. Meditate on this vortex. Bring forward those in your life who you are having difficulty with. Bring them *into* this vortex during your meditation. Look at them through new eyes. See through the illusion; see the play and the part they are playing. Then you can release and send them unconditional love. That is all you need to do to release yourself. Because while you continue to hold resentment and anger or any negative intensity within you, you cannot be free.

And you know what? You hold the key. You! Not the person who created all that anger or hurt, no. It's you! As long as you choose to hold onto it, to feed it occasionally through reliving a part of it in your mind, giving it more energy, then you continue to give that person your power. It is you who makes the choice. You and only you hold the power. But there is a great power in release.

This is the final, and perhaps the most difficult lesson to overcome for mankind—the emotional body. You have the power, not your emotions. You control your emotions through choice—your choice. Use the Thymus Vortex. It is a very fine, yet oh so powerful vibrational energy.

The Soul Star

The Soul Star Vortex unites your right and left brains to the Pineal and Pituitary Glands. Some call this the third brain. Yet you must remember that you still have a human body and therefore cannot remain in the higher realms all of the time. If you do others will find it difficult to communicate with you. You won't hear everything they say to you. My husband Michael sometimes asks me, "Where are you?" Of course I'm on another dimension, usually having a great conversation with Kuthumi, while I'm still physically conscious. As above, so below.

The colour of the Soul Star vortex is magenta edged in gold. You connect fully to the Soul plane and all who reside there. Speaking to loved ones who have crossed is not difficult at this level. This is the eighth vortex and is an important gateway to the universal energies and spirit. It intertwines greatly with the physical body forming a wonderful braided 'rope' between the two. It connects you to all that is.

The Earth Star

We are multi dimensional beings and this is a classic example. We need to remember to ground ourselves too. Imagine roots coming out from your feet and going down deep into the Earth through the Earth Star Vortex. Mmm, I need to explain this one don't I? This vortex lies about twelve inches below your feet in your Etheric body, as all the vortexes do. The Earth Star Vortex also connects you to mother Earth. Visualizing those roots going down deep into the Earth will 'pull' your awareness back to physical reality. If you feel 'spacey' you will need to do this simple exercise. We are learning to balance the energies.

But back to the Soul Star Vortex. I call this vortex God's elevator because it takes you straight through to the higher realms very quickly when you learn to understand and use it properly. Of course as there is no time on the higher dimensions or realms, everything happens in a split second of our linear time. You can meditate for what seems like a short time but when you look at your clock an hour could have passed. You have been visiting 'no time.'

You may have noticed that you are fast running out of time each day to do your chores and work. This is because as mankind en mass is raising his vibration; we are entering 'no time' more and more. We are functioning in the higher realms more than we realize which affects our sense of time. When you begin to work more in the higher realms through these higher vortexes everything changes.

The Christ Consciousness

The Christ Consciousness Vortex represents another gateway to the Gateway to the Sun. This has a higher meaning. At this level you connect more consciously to God Consciousness, the Sun representing the higher heart of God. You are able to connect easily to past, present and future time lines. You understand the aspects of yourself and also that of connectiveness. You heal your traumas of soul. You are able to connect to the Space Brotherhood, and again realize there is so much more. What you see with your physical eyes is not all there is at all. There are other worlds and other beings of Light beyond us that do exist. You see why I call it another gateway.

Cosmic Gateway Vortex

You can experience quite a journey in conscious awareness to reach this Cosmic Gateway. You again release, grow, learn and finally stand in awe as you reach yet another new level of understanding. At this point, when you are able to fully work with this Christ Conscious Vortex, you are aware of all of your seven bodies, the great time lines of space, you understand the various levels of energy, and above all, you fully see the great illusion each one takes part in throughout your life in order for you to experience and grow. What could we call this?

The Dance of the Divine. Yes, sounds good to me.

The Galactic

The next Vortex is the Galactic Vortex. You now move onto solar awareness, Galactic awareness. Yet another higher gateway. The colour is peach/gold/magenta. You will by now incorporate all of your energy vortexes so far. You are now able to access knowledge of the Cosmos and the Divine. Here you begin to connect to even higher and much larger Divine energy. At this point now you have become a very high dimensional being of Light. Your life would have changed a great deal. You would have changed a great deal. You would begin to glow. Others may note a radiance of your skin, particularly around the face. You need to do this as you will have learnt to sustain a much higher vibration of energy.

You are still connected to your physical body of course. Yet you are preparing on a Soul level to end this cycle of existence. Your Light body must be kept strong and clean to buffer the higher levels of energy now emerging on Earth.

On the physical level you now find that many of your 'trinkets' no longer hold the joy and pleasure for you that they once did. You once held them close but no longer need to. You finally begin to understand they are only part of your creation. Only yours to have for a short time of this existence on Earth. You enjoy them with a new awareness now. An awareness of knowing they really are unimportant in the bigger scheme of things.

It is that which you cannot hold physically which is your true treasure. When you connect from the Galactic Vortex you see this and acknowledge it without emotion. It merely 'is.' You now exist in harmony with yourself at this level. You must achieve this first. Harmony with others will then simply flow. You function in balance having experienced diversity of total duality of everything you know.

Physical wants and needs, love and hate, persecution and glory, cold and heat, poverty and riches, controller and victim, the abuser and the abused, slave and freedom, malnourished and obese, heavy energy and fine energy, lower state of being and higher state of being—all. Yet through it all you come back to one single thing which transcends all—love. Through love we learn to overcome, to grow, to move forward as Light Beings.

The Universal Gateway

The Universal Gateway Vortex is the final vortex /chakra we will look at here. It is yet another gateway known as the Universal gateway. It is here you are able to function in parallel Universes going through wormholes to new worlds. You can travel freely in spirit form everywhere and anywhere you choose. Though in saying this snooping on someone is very frowned upon by the hierarchy of spirit. This is considered misuse of power.

But we often seek freedom from our 'heavy' physical bodies. You can also connect with others from your soul family group. Recognition is easy. You 'see' on all levels. You feel all. You fully remember who you are, your power, your Light. You now merge freely with Divine Light as you choose. You understand how you need to nourish your being with Light energy frequently. You see it all—in an instant! You communicate freely with other Light beings and spirit guides. Not just from this Universe, but from the Universe next to ours as well.

You may not be able to comprehend all of this expansion of you. This great understanding of just who you really are. But I know you will, one day. Because more and more people will begin talking about it. Right now it's called Quantum Physics. I'm here to tell you it's so much more. Scientists are beginning to understand. Some of you need that reassurance. Others simply know and trust.

For too long now man has given his mind precedence over everything. This is not the answer. Words such as trust and faith have almost been forgotten. Many are out of balance. It is time for mankind to connect to his Heart Vortex, and the higher heart, the Thymus Vortex. This is the only way forward. Master Kuthumi has said this many times.

Right now mankind is unhappy, going round and round in circles of despair. The Light Beings are standing by; repeating their messages in various terminologies but the meaning remains the same. They are patiently waiting. Waiting for man to wake up. To realize you must connect to your heart, connect to unconditional love. Only then we may come back into balance and be ready to access the higher levels of awareness, of being, of existence.

Connected to All That Is

All the Vortexes are connected of course. All interact and carry various levels of energy. We are on a great journey this life time. A great awakening of Soul. With each step you take you are able to hold more Light and gain more strength. To let go and release that which no longer serves you.

Chapter Eighteen

Your Many Bodies

What an amazing journey we've been on. The Chinese, Native Americans and Indian cultures all knew of the Chakra system, which I call the Vortexes due to their shape, not unlike a cone. C.W.Leadbeater wrote about it quite openly in the early nineteen hundreds. This was the beginning for many to understand the human energy system.

You also have outer bodies as well which are unseen by the physical eyes. The outer bodies also relate to your higher awareness. There are seven bodies. Now in your expanded awareness you really see the true meaning of the phrase, as above, so below.

The Physical Body

The **first** body is of course the physical body. You can see and touch your body. You know you have skin, bones, organs, cells and nerves. Yet as we, Master Kuthumi and I have shown you, there are higher energy vortexes which really govern your health as well. You may think that it all begins with your physical body. After all, this is what you can see and feel isn't it? It's actually the final 'body' to receive various energies, even illness.

Illness begins in your outer bodies and filters through to your physical body and consciousness. That is why the Lemurian exercise Master Kuthumi gave some years ago is so important. The meditation strengthens the outer bodies in your auric field and is still available on the website. Your Aura consists of your outer bodies with colour and energy constantly moving through. If you have an Aura photograph taken, then another, you will see the colours change from one to the other. This is because of the various energies and your emotions which flow in and through your auric field constantly and this makes the colours change. Those who have a strong Light quotient will show a lot of white light in the photo. Spirit guides also show as masses or circles of white Light. They are usually quite distinct.

It is in the physical body where you feel pain. The physical body is a dense energy and you can really feel the density and heaviness when you come back from a deep mediation as you re-enter the physical body. It is the heavy matter of the physical body you feel.

The Etheric Body

The **second** body is known as the Etheric body which lies very close to your physical body. It is a replica of your physical body, cell for cell, organ for organ, and bone for bone. But you can't see this body with physical eyes. If you lose a limb you can still feel it being a part of your body for weeks afterwards. That's because it exists also in your Etheric body which must also adjust to the loss. The Etheric is in many ways a buffer for the physical body. Colours and Light move freely through this body. The Etheric also connects to electromagnetic energies.

The new Crystalline Grid is sensed here. The healing field of crystals works with this body as well. The electromagnetic energy is as vital to us as the air we all breathe. The energies of the Sun through the Solar Flares affect this body also. The Etheric is the blueprint for the physical body.

The Emotional Body

The **third** body is the Emotional Body. This is the lower emotional Body. It is here you hold all emotional blockages. The resentments, anger and turmoil. Master Kuthumi has said constantly the Emotional Body is man's biggest challenge to overcome. This is so true. It really is this body that holds you back from moving onto higher levels of awareness and ascension. Many become stuck on this level until they 'get it.' It's when you see you simply have to do the work yourself, the clearing of this body, that you really begin to move forward.

The Emotional Body is where you hold your feelings on how you see yourself too. Where your darkest secrets and fears are kept. To ascend to the Light this 'cupboard' must be cleared out. Again, once you see most of these are old paradigms of behaviour you feel you can then finally release quite freely. Thankfully this wanting to clear comes with your higher awareness. As you learn to control your fears you begin to let go. Remember a lot of your fears have been locked inside for most of your life. And that's it isn't it? When we fear something we tend to lock it away. To not look at it, but an experience may bring it out which reminds ourselves it's still there, hiding.

But at this point in this book, you now have a new understanding. But let's go to the three essentials in any relationship—REVEAL—WANTS—NEEDS. As you look at your Emotional Body, you are also looking at your relationship with yourself. How do you see yourself now? Are you weak, strong, do you like yourself? You hopefully did some work on this so I ask you to do more work on this now because you have reached a new awareness. Ask yourself these questions. Really get down to the nitty gritty and be honest. Reveal *exactly* how you now see yourself and how you *feel* about yourself.

Next, ask about your wants. Not your material wants. We're looking at your Emotional Body here. If you want to be happy, to feel freedom and joy then you need to look deep inside your 'emotional cupboard.' Is it empty? Is it clear? If it's not, and be honest, stop right now. Get out your STOP sign—where is it? Don't put this off. Take out that old issue, take out that old fear, and take out that old pain.

> ## They all belong to your past!

They don't belong to the **new you!** Neither does the cave or the cave language! The first step is to forgive yourself. So often with past hurts there is a part of you that feels you deserve to suffer and to be in pain so you hold onto that pain tightly. Once you forgive yourself, once you understand—it's done. Then you can step into forgiveness. You forgive yourself first. Forgiving others will follow. Clear your 'emotional cupboard.' Think only positive thoughts.

My mother used to say," If you can't say something nice, then don't say anything at all."
That's what you need to focus on. Doing this clearing work will also help you to hold more of the Light energy and to feel stronger. To be more peaceful and content with yourself. You can be. You *can* create that space within yourself.

The Mental Body

The **fourth** body is the Mental Body. Your conscious mind relates directly to the Mental Body. Your very thoughts—and there is no such thing as an idle thought. You create from your thoughts. Now that's a scary thought! We need to retrain our new thinking manner in order to survive.

Do you remember that wonderful word—delete? Use it. If you can catch yourself thinking a negative thought, STOP and say DELETE! It's very powerful. Very soon you will discover you are using that delete word less and less. Your thoughts will have become more positive. Any negative behaviour you notice is observed and deleted. You become the observer.

When you notice someone else's negative behaviour you have a choice to make. Are you going to give it any of *your* energy? And if so, in what way? You see the observer sees, knows, understands and steps away when necessary. It's not about winning. It's about the journey. So it's good to retrain your thoughts. This will not only uplift your Mental Body, but your actions as well.

All of the bodies we have discussed so far are heavier lower bodies connected to the physical world. As you journey toward enlightenment you seek to transcend those heavier energies.

The Higher Emotional Body

The **fifth** body is the Higher Emotional Body. This is the mid way point. The gateway to becoming a Being of Light. Able to feel, see and work in the Light energy. The energy of the Divine. Some call this Universal energy. Again, terminology. This body is filled with glorious colour. The more balanced you are and the more you have cleared your other bodies, then the more vibrant the colours will be. Your physical body will be healthier too. You feel good.

But—there's one catch! The colours radiate out merging not only with all your bodies, but also other people's bodies. These are often strangers you walk past in the shopping mall or at work. Just as your colours merge into their energy field, some of theirs merges into yours as well. These represent emotions. Have you ever gone shopping, feeling great, and arrived back home, got in the front door and for no reason you feel angry. Very angry. You need to understand that someone else's anger has filtered into your Auric field and that's what you are experiencing, someone else's anger. What can you do? Cleanse—right away. Don't let the anger manifest too strongly. Know that anger will stay and grow til you cleanse your auric field and get rid of it. You need to go into a light meditative state and cleanse yourself. You could use the Violet Ray of Transformation on page 182.

This is also a reminder to cleanse your bodies often. Keep yourself strong—all of you. This is important because this body connects to your spirit guides energy. It is a 'feeling' body. You become aware of the finer energies, the energies of spirit and of God. This body also brings in feelings of compassion and Grace.

The Higher Mental Body

The Higher Mental Body rises above your conscious mind. It lifts from your conscious will to Divine Will. It is here where you choose to surrender your lower will. With a higher understanding this is done willingly. You are choosing love and peace over control and materiality. *You* choose. And those are the key words here—*you choose*. No one says you *have* to, or you *should* do it. You choose.

At this point you are advancing on your evolutionary path. You desire peace in your life and unconditional love so you open your heart vortex and allow it to flow with your higher heart, your Soul. This keeps you strong, vibrant and happy. In this state you can flow with even more Soul Light. This filters down through your bodies to the physical and you consciously register it as a feeling of 'bliss.' We have one more body to go.

The Body of Divinity

The **seventh** body is the body of Divinity. Sometimes called Oneness, or the Divine Mind. You are at one here and feel complete. You vibrate at a very high frequency of energy. Those looking at your auric field would see such a glowing Light. The Light would often merge with a golden Light. You have become a being of Light here, and are able to hold and maintain great Light energy. This Light protects you from any lower energies wishing to enter your auric field. You seek Divine guidance in all things. You now live in complete peace because you choose to and you don't like anything of a negative energy around you. You know because you are aware of all energy so you feel it instantly. You move gently, seeking a higher path in all undertakings of your daily life. You are connected 24/7, yet are able to walk between the Dimensions.

Now—We Finally Get It!

This is our path at this time on Earth. To help each other and the Earth transcend to a higher vibration of being. Once we reach this point of understanding, of Grace, we won't go back. Why would we want to go back to war, hatred and greed? But it has had purpose. Because now we have experienced all levels we can fully understand. We get it! There is no curiosity and no need to experience a negative state again. So we feel secure and blissfully happy, connected fully to the Divine Consciousness, all One.

Master Kuthumi tells me this time there is an even higher body working with a higher state of awareness. But we are not ready for this entire knowledge yet. It will be given as the new Earth and new ways of being become mankind's reality. Some souls are beginning to move into their eighth body. Others merely think they are, yet they are not. This is all part of opening and growing into the eighth body. It is where we will all function in the higher dimensions in a fully raised consciousness, seeing and being with all.

So mankind journeys forward in Light, growing and evolving. What a wonderful journey it is. When you choose to change you willingly change your attitude. Your own spirit guides and angels come around to help and guide you, always with total unconditional love. As you grow in awareness, as you clear your lower bodies, you awaken to their energies. You begin to see signs on your path. It may be a book given to you which awakens you further, or you notice a synchronicity of events which have the power to open a big new door—if you don't allow yourself to succumb to lower fear and doubt. These are your challenges. To see the unseen, to listen to the hidden messages and to see the sign posts on the way, all given by spirit. To be aware on a whole new level—your sixth sense is finally awake!

In the first chapter I asked you to write four things you would like to change about yourself. How have you gone with these? If you haven't completed all four of them yet, please begin another list now. This book has given you so many tools to make it easier for you to open new doors for yourself. The most exciting thing of all is that you're the one who benefits. No one else.

Know you're worth it!

Oh yes you are indeed, so begin now. Don't put it off. That's just cheating yourself.

You Are the Creator Now

Do you now see yourself as a creator? Do you see you create your life every day? You may think it's your boss or your partner but it's not. It's you. Because you choose. What you think, do and say—all of it. You don't have to agree with another. You don't have to argue either. You choose what 'space,' and what 'body' you will operate from and how you will respond to another. No one else controls that. There are no victims. To tell yourself repeatedly you are a victim simply binds you in despair and hopelessness. You're in the cave; in fact you're a cave dweller with this mind set. Is this really where you want to be? You have the power within to change. But *you* must take the first step! *You* must choose. So get your CAN DO button out. Where is it anyway? Relegated to a dark drawer? I hope not.

That's fine if you've outgrown him, but have you really? You know you haven't outgrown him til you're operating from your seventh body. Until then use that button as often as you need to. Use your Wish Board too. Make a new one. Why not? Create what you want in your life.

The electromagnetic fields are changing, just as we are changing. Our DNA continues to change which in turn allows us to hold more Light particles within. Keep your Light body strong. The Light body resides within your Aura connecting with the Etheric body. This helps you communicate on the various dimensional levels. A strong Light body will keep your physical body stronger as well because illness cannot pass through a strong auric field very well at all. You may feel a heaviness sitting in your auric field. You may feel it as anger. Clear it. Clean it out. Just as you keep your physical body clean, so you need to keep the Etheric body clean as well. We all have the ability to renew ourselves from within.

> **Forgive, Release, Cleanse,
> Love yourself.**

Begin listening to your inner feelings. Some call this a 'gut' feeling. What are you drawn to? Listen and watch. Begin to expand your own sixth sense. Start to feel the different energies too. By developing your sixth sense and becoming aware you will begin to see and hear your spirit guides more. So many people allow the ego self through the conscious mind to step in and lead you away from your higher knowledge. Be on guard, always. You cannot destroy the ego self. You need it for survival. But beware of egotism.

After a while you will realize you are actually listening to your higher self, your own intuition. You are noticing all sorts of signs from spirit that you never noticed before. That's how it begins. It's really not so difficult, you are spirit after all. You just need to be aware, to listen and to feel. You are opening to a wonderful new world. It's so exciting! Just don't leave it too late.

> **You are loved before you are born
> This is forgotten at birth**
>
> **So why do you need to work
> so hard to love yourself?**
>
> **Trust and believe who
> you truly are.**

About The Author

Lynette has been working with the Ascended Masters and Arch Angels for over 25 years. The Kuthumi School of Wisdom website houses many channelled teachings and meditations to help people raise their vibrational energy and gain higher wisdom. The wisdom the ancient Wise Ones have always known—now given to you.

www.kuthumischool.com